Estela

Estela

ignacio mattos

with gabe ulla

photographs by marcus nilsson

Artisan | New York

Library of Congress Cataloging-in-Publication Data

Names: Mattos, Ignacio, author | Ulla, Gabe, author. | Nilsson, Marcus
    (Photographer) author.
Title: Estela / Ignacio Mattos with Gabe Ulla ; photographs by
    Marcus Nilsson.
Description: New York, NY : Artisan, a division of Workman Publishing
    Company, Inc., [2018] | Includes an index.
 Identifiers: LCCN 2018024625 | ISBN 9781579656706 (hardcover :
 alk. paper)
Subjects: LCSH: Cooking. | Quick and easy cooking. | Estela
    (Restaurant) | LCGFT: Cookbooks.
Classification: LCC TX714 .M3398 2018 | DDC 641.5/12—dc23
LC record available at https://lccn.loc.gov/2018024625

Cover and book design by James Casey
Cover photographs by Marcus Nilsson

. Artisan books are available at special discounts when purchased in
bulk for premiums and sales promotions as well as for fund-raising or
educational use. Special editions or book excerpts also can be created
to specification. For details, contact the Special Sales Director at the
address below, or send an e-mail to specialmarkets@workman.com.

For speaking engagements, contact
speakersbureau@workman.com.

Published by Artisan
A division of Workman Publishing Co., Inc.
225 Varick Street
New York, NY 10014-4381
artisanbooks.com

Artisan is a registered trademark of
Workman Publishing Co., Inc.

Published simultaneously in Canada by
Thomas Allen & Son, Limited

Printed in China
First printing, October 2018

10 9 8 7 6 5 4 3 2 1

contents

an immigrant cooking

I've never been too comfortable talking about my cooking because I hope, in a way, that it can speak for itself. That has always been the idea, making food that doesn't require much explanation to convey emotion.

That said, of course there's a story behind it.

I'm from Uruguay, a country with a history of colonialism and immigration, the story of many places. In our case, because of eradication, we lack the rich indigenous representation of other South American nations. Nowadays, we're three million or so people and twelve million cows. It's a quite progressive society, and even though the country is smaller and less populous than the state of Utah, we claim the glory of two World Cup soccer championships. Still, many of us are born with a chip on our shoulders: There's not much mathematical logic to the successes we've had, and our neighbors are more famous than we are. More than anything, though, I'd say that Uruguayans have a distinctly noble, humble, and laid-back way about them that resonates.

Growing up in a small town outside of Montevideo and a short drive from my family's farm was a pretty ideal environment for a kid like me. Between endless adventures—canoeing, fishing, hitchhiking on trains, stealing apples from another family's orchard—and some not-so-wonderful family moments, we'd always have to be on time for meals. On weekends, we'd do long lunches and *asados* (barbecues), when we'd eat all kinds of meat. During the week, my grandmother Ercilia would handle most of the cooking, but sometimes my mother would take over for her. Ercilia had her staples: hand-rolled pastas, *milanesas*, *pasqualinas*, tortillas, mostly recipes in the Spanish and Italian tradition since that is her heritage. To this day, I don't think she has ever followed a recipe. We all gravitated toward the kitchen, and, as it is in most families, we had to do our part, either to set the table, grate cheese, or, of course, wash the dishes. Most of the time, I would be responsible for making the salad. I never saw this as a chore; I'd get an idea from a homemaking manual and then prepare it my way, doing the best I could.

The table was where everything happened: where we talked about family issues, annoying town gossip, and politics. There were often heated discussions and arguments but not what I would necessarily call dialogues. Pretty frequently, the situation would heat up and at times even blow up, but everyone would stick around to finish the meal and forget it ever happened. I would later discover that this kind of dysfunction wasn't limited to us Latins. The table is where I had my first glass of wine outside of a church. This wasn't because it was offered to me but because I found my way to it. Drinking a splash of wine was fine with my family, but as I grew up, my persistence on other matters and what you could call my "idiosyncrasies" could get me into trouble, especially in a small town where there wasn't much room for a bored teenager, where being even the slightest bit weird was discouraged. Eventually, finding a way out was quite easy: At sixteen, I got shown the way out.

The early part of the journey was made up of nights on the beds and couches of dear friends (some random ones, too), in backseats of cars, on many lonely bus and train rides. I enrolled in culinary school mostly because it was familiar: For years, I had given my mother, Gloria, and my grandmother a break in the kitchen. And I recalled that someone, somewhere, had said to me that I could do the work anywhere I wanted. (I had considered art school, as well as a professional soccer career, but I had always struggled following rules and I didn't have any figures in my life to motivate me on either of those paths, anyway.) My first experiences were in questionable kitchens run by people whom I got on with fine, but whose work was not driven by passion and certainly not by love.

Then I met Michel Kerever. I had no idea who he was. He had been hired by the hotel in Montevideo where Mónica—who worked at the office of my culinary school and I think noticed my initiative—sent me to intern. The first French person I had ever met, Kerever was also the first person who wasn't "working" but doing what he loved, the first true chef. Tens of thousands of miles from Paris, he was in his element, wearing a shirt and tie under his white chef's coat, with perfectly shined shoes (not a look I ever aspired to, but his disciplined style struck me). He would arch himself forward and dive his entire head into steaming pots and pans to get a sense of how a soup was coming along, shouting in a language that no one around him understood but that really appealed to me. It wasn't just the smelling and tasting; it was the way he looked, touched, listened, and felt in a frantic way that was anything but random. It was his posture and a stare, when he would press his glasses to his face, that told you he could see and sense everything around him. It was his commitment and intensity. Most of the times that I tried to do more than I was told to, he'd bat my hand away. But one morning when he disappeared to charm so-and-so, I flipped the vegetables for his ratatouille and *tournéed* vegetables. He came back, and to his surprise, I did these tasks well, and he commended me with a *"Très bien"* followed by, this time, an encouraging tap. This is when I decided that for me cooking would never be work, and I should make abundantly clear that it never has been since.

I had no idea who Francis Mallmann was, either, but Mónica sent me to Los Negros, his restaurant in the popular Uruguayan beach town of José Ignacio. It was perhaps the most beautiful of his places. Francis, in his way, described it recently as "a shabby palace of grace." He had a fun record collection and an impressive library that included first editions from all sorts of writers, many that I already loved, as well as works by the British cookbook author Elizabeth David, which I had never read before and took me to countries I had never been. I was embraced by the intimate group of people who worked there every single day and began, for the first time in a kitchen, to develop a sense of belonging. At Los Negros, we'd do everything ourselves—bake bread, make desserts, clean the kitchen. I'd sleep in the restaurant, wake up, and, over

coffee and a book, watch the ocean before moving back into the routine.

I consider Francis my main mentor. I learned his cooking inside and out and can still do most, if not all, of it from memory. I worked for him during a transitional period, when he was moving away from a more classic French style and embracing the elemental approach he is known for today. Beyond providing me with a cooking foundation and a way of working that was both structured and relaxed, Francis gave me the chance to see the world. We did stuff that most rational people would not: We staged an outdoor event during a major snowstorm in New York when everyone thought that we were going to cancel; built a big fire on a rooftop in SoHo that caused a neighbor to come outside of his penthouse apartment while still in his underwear and scold us (Francis won him over and we ended up feeding him); and cooked on top of a mountain in Mendoza for some kind of prince and other "notables," including Peter Kaminsky, a great writer who has done a couple of books with Francis and who later introduced me to Donna Lennard of the beloved Il Buco in New York City, where I would eventually spend a good chunk of time cooking Italian and Mediterranean food and learning about incredible ingredients in the region.

Francis is the person who arranged for me to work at a place called Zuni Café, in San Francisco. Once again, I knew very little to nothing about it. This was when communication wasn't what it is today, and I didn't have much planned for the trip, aside from exploring my interest in the Beat Generation, seeing some bands, and eating at Chez Panisse, which somehow by then I did know about. The morning I arrived at Zuni Café, Judy Rodgers warmly welcomed me. She gave me a quick tour of the kitchen and took me to the bar for an espresso. With my limited English, I asked that I start right away. She agreed. At Zuni, I discovered an eclectic and versatile style of cooking, driven by Judy's focused, obsessive approach and grounded in the abundance of California's products. She would come and go and whisper little tips on cooking in my ear, like how to move my fingers while dressing a salad and how to taste in a very thoughtful, determined way, all in the greatest level of detail.

Later, I had the chance to spend time at Chez Panisse, which has served as the school for many great chefs, including Judy herself. It was eye-opening to live what Alice Waters created there, a community where everyone collectively contributed to her vision. I got to work with some of the most experienced cooks I've ever met, like David Tanis, with his effortless style, who became a lifelong friend; and Jean-Pierre Moullé, with his discerning palate and reassuring, confident presence, who not only encouraged me to trust my senses but was also one of the first chefs to articulate a major compliment to me. And how could I forget Gilbert Pilgram, a key member in the Chez and Zuni worlds? He was the one who believed in me enough to let me cut the line and join the kitchen, which was certainly a challenge at the beginning.

My first travels outside of kitchens also played a decisive role. There were my initial visits to Europe, or the Old Continent, as we refer to it in South America: through Italy, where I was attracted to the unfussy and satisfying *cucina povera*; to France, which at the time was still considered the pinnacle of gastronomy; and to Spain, which in the early 2000s was establishing itself as a major culinary destination. I spent plenty of time in Galicia, in northwestern Spain, which is where my aunt Ana and cousins live. Every morning, we would go to the markets, and part of the routine included a beer or sherry on the way back home, which must have been no later than 10:30. This was not too different from the way we did it back home, but the quality of the product was much higher. In Galicia, you can find some of the best seafood anywhere. I remember eating the boiled octopus and potatoes, *pulpo a feira*, at a street market and being stunned. And the *lacón con grelos*, or salt-cured ham shoulder boiled with turnip greens and potatoes, has stayed with me as a reference for absurdly perfect comfort food. So has the *tortilla española*—good potatoes, good eggs, and good onions—that I grew up eating at home at least once or even twice a week. But it wasn't all rustic: By then I had saved up for many high-end meals, one of the most memorable of which was at Mugaritz, outside of San Sebastian. There, Andoni Luis Aduriz was cooking food that pushed boundaries but was still simple to the eye and deeply connected to his heritage.

Between all these trips from north to south, east to west, south to north, and north to south again, working in different cities and visiting friends and family, I managed to spend some time in Brazil. This vast country offered me an energy and variety of perspectives that I had no access to growing up. It may sound stupid, but the mere act of tasting a good mango or banana for the first time was fascinating. I tried the little-known food of Bahia, in the north, a cultural mecca that is the home of the Afro-Brazilian community. With its dishes like the fish stew *moqueca*, the deep-fried beans *acarejé*, and *vatapá*, a creamy paste made of shrimp and coconut milk, this cuisine is perhaps my favorite. And it was in Brazil that I met the mother of my son, Paco.

New York eventually became home. Very easily, as many who have ended up here can tell you; it's a generous town, and there's a great fulfillment that comes from being a part of it—the sense of community, the nerve the city breeds in you, the drive that most of us share. This is where I met Thomas Carter, who was looking for his next project at the same time I was. He knew of a space downtown that had previously been a sports bar. I knew it in its previous incarnation as the Knitting Factory music venue. There was nothing fancy or grand about it. There were a lot of cons, actually, but we decided that we loved the location and wanted to make it work.

As we got to know each other, Thomas and I kept talking about New York institutions like Balthazar, the now-extinct Florent, and Prune and places in Europe like the Barcelona tavern Cal Pep and the Paris bistro Le Chateaubriand—restaurants that were serious yet accessible and fun, that could serve as your neighborhood spot for a drink and a dish but could also be more than that.

We wanted our place to have its own identity. As for the food, I wrestled with myself and slowly molded my approach, figuring out how I could give people what they wanted in a way that they didn't expect, in a way that was true to myself and true to my journey and the many voices that were part of it. I would cook like an immigrant who comes from a country of immigrants working in a city of immigrants in a country

of immigrants. The food had to have nerve. It needed to be assertive, and if far from perfect, it would still bare the soul. Even if you were numb, it would shake you up a little bit, a kind of cooking that would connect in the same way some pieces of music do from the moment you first hear them. Some of it would sound or look common. Some of it would look or sound alien. Yet all of it would feel good and disarm and perhaps make you realize, at one point or another, that you'd never tried anything like it.

notes on my cooking

One of the few rules I allow myself to follow is that the product should always dictate the direction. This requires a certain discernment, an understanding of the ingredients: sensing, looking, smelling, touching, and tasting, all in a synchronous manner. Do not let any of this intimidate you, as it should be a fun and delicious process that allows you to develop your palate and build a library of flavors. Here I will offer a description of how I approach cooking, from sourcing to serving.

Sight can tell you a lot before you even taste. In some cases, you will be able to see immediately if a fruit or vegetable is underripe, fresh, or spoiled. If it is smashed, for instance, you will know already that it will not be the best choice for a salad. The interior "cells" will be crushed and it will not have the same effect on the palate. But it can be blended with other fruits or vegetables to make a juice. If it's just ripe, it will have the proper acidity. When it comes to fruit, "just ripe" will always be my choice, because you want it to be sweet, but not too sweet, and you want it firm for it to play the correct role in a salad. When fruit is overripe, the sugars in the fruit turn and sweeten. Such fruit would be good for a sorbet base or a marmalade.

Touch and taste the products; be curious and even a bit insolent in the face of resistance from the farmer or supplier. Most of the time, they'll offer samples out of a sense of pride, so you should have no problem. But if you do, simply apologize and do it again. It works. In my case, I can just fall back on "No speak English."

Then we have the tactile sense, which you'll utilize at the same time that you're observing — if the item is firm, if it has give, the way it feels in your hand, its density, its general structure. And also at the same time is its smell, the intensity of the fragrance.

All of this leads us to taste. When you taste, learn to isolate and focus. Be attentive to how ingredients taste individually. Taste each one raw when possible, and then perhaps cook a piece or two to understand how it changes.

See how it feels when you eat it, how that feeling affects how it actually tastes, how it eats. Do this a couple of times. You can try this with pretty much all ingredients.

An apple is a simple and quite fascinating example for tasting. There's the snap of the peel and your teeth cutting into the flesh, the juices that flow in every direction, the sound of the bite in your head. Each bite feels new, with variables upon variables to each one — and indeed, to each variety of apple, if you want to get carried away with all possibilities. In every case, however, you derive a sense of fulfillment from getting to the core, at least until the moment you realize you want more. This feeling is something I try to achieve in every dish.

In some strange, purist way, my responsibility is to preserve the characteristics of the ingredients, playing with them just enough to take them where you might not expect, making minimal touches that elevate.

layering, tension, and balance

My goal is to build layers of flavor and to find a harmonious, happy place just at the borderline of too much. It's about creating a certain tension that makes the dish vibrant, almost electric. A few important factors go into creating this effect.

You will probably notice that we often use more than one vinegar at a time, as well as lemon and grapefruit zest and subtle sources of heat like the pickling liquid of Thai chiles. Fish sauce and juiced green garlic, though not immediately detectable, add complexity to different preparations. So do juiced greens and herbs in certain salads and other dishes, also bringing brightness in a way that sometimes can be more appealing and satisfying than encountering pieces of those ingredients. We pay attention also to the particular darkness—the shading—we give to nuts and bread when charring, as it can impact the direction of a dish, as well as to the manner in which we toast and grind certain spices to impart flavor and fragrance.

To build flavor, time is important for ingredients like meats or some vegetables, either through brining, marinating, curing, or air-drying. Yes, we try to preserve the natural qualities of the product, but at the same time, we try to amplify them, perhaps with an assertive seasoning blend or by lacquering as we cook. But it's important to adjust the intensity of the cooking based on the product: gentle and slow for cod, for example, and more aggressive for monkfish and pork, which can handle it. We do get a bit serious about this at the restaurant, because it's essential to how the product will end up making diners feel when they eat it.

Once served, mains usually sit in a nurturing broth, which you might call a sauce, though it's lighter. Or in the case of beef, we'll pair it with a robust and sultry condiment made with Taleggio. We live for these sauces, and there's nothing more satisfying than soaking them up at the end of a dish.

how it eats

Everything from how you slice a particular vegetable or piece of bread to the way you treat each element affects how the dish will eat. Even the order in which you introduce seasonings can determine how it feels on the palate. Above all, it must not only taste good but also be pleasant on the palate.

plating and appearance

Part of me is extremely visual, and yet part of me is tempted to say that I don't place too much importance on presentation, because I think we can all agree that elaborate aesthetics don't always translate to deliciousness. But for a number of reasons, I do care about the way a dish looks. Therefore, we strive for a clean aesthetic, defined by plenty of circles and the veiling of ingredients. In most cases, this is meant to give people who are eating in a dark, noisy room a sense of discovery when they've been served what appears to be a monotonous-looking arrangement, which might prompt them to ask, "Really, a pile of endive leaves?" However, once they move one or two of those leaves around to reveal the croutons and cheese at the bottom, it's like finding a twenty-dollar bill in your shirt pocket. Our plating can also influence how something eats, as it allows us to arrange the ingredients so that the diner gets the exact mouthfuls we want him or her to have. It's as true for the endives (see page 85) as it is for the tartare (see page 79), which at first looks like a pile of raw beef but is actually the result of mixing the ingredients together to ensure that every forkful has the right amount of crunch, acid, meat, elderberry, and onion, leaving minimal room for error. In some ways, it's a childlike approach, but I'm okay with that.

how to cook from this book

I truly believe that all you need is an appetite and a willingness to jump in, and that there is no reason to feel intimidated, but here's some guidance. My first recommendation would be to read through the book and get a sense of the cooking. Pick out the recipes that you could probably execute without much of a challenge. There may be a lot of them. For some, this may mean a dish from the Snacks section, and that is completely fine, because you may end up with the best egg salad or cocktail almonds you've ever made. The sauces and condiments in Supporting Players are versatile and mostly quite quick to cook, and the Brunch toasts and egg dishes are memorable. For others, though, the entry point could be a challenge in multiple stages, like our classic *arroz negro* (which isn't even that hard once you've prepared all the components). I find that our salads, though not your typical versions, are particularly friendly. As long as you have the ingredients handy, your chances of screwing them up are minimal.

In general, I'd say to embrace repetition. There's great satisfaction in mastering a technique or full recipe, no matter how simple, and this will help build your confidence as you move on to less familiar territory. We all know that if you want to get good at something, doing it again and again is the only way. Remember, also, that you don't need to commit to a complete recipe. Not at all: You may prefer to home in on certain ideas or techniques and then incorporate those approaches into your own cooking. This could be how we dress and layer salads, or how we treat fish, quail, pork, and beef. This may actually happen, also, if you don't have access to an ingredient or two, so you shouldn't let those situations discourage you.

If a particular serving portion looks too small to feed four or more, simply double it. For the most part, these recipes reflect how we do things at the restaurant, where diners are encouraged to pass around plates and try as many different dishes as possible, instead of limiting each guest at a table to an appetizer and one entrée. As for the Mains section, they are "traditional" serving sizes, and you'll probably have to figure out what to do with the leftovers.

Again, if certain ingredients are out of reach, don't worry. In some cases, I offer information on substitutions when available, and researching online can be extremely helpful as well. I would only insist that you be selective about the products you source, as it really will impact the final result. Remember, the less packaging, the better.

Finally, worry as much or as little as you wish about plating and how a dish ultimately looks. If you'd rather serve a recipe that calls for two or four plates on one large plate or platter, go for it. And if you don't want to use the ring molds, don't worry about it. I do this for a living.

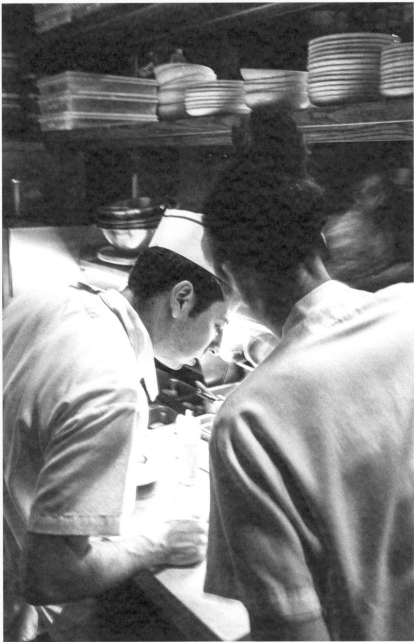

estela
essent

I like the idea of not having too many fancy gadgets. In fact, you may already have some of these tools in your own kitchen. And if you don't, they're pretty

ials

easy to obtain. Same goes for most of the pantry staples listed in this section, which should give you a sense of the flavors we favor.

tools

a good black pan

Cast iron is great if you already have one, but we like carbon steel because it is lighter and easier to handle.

cake tester

To test the doneness of meat, I prefer the old-fashioned approach of inserting a cake tester into the center of the protein and then pressing it to the bottom of your lip. You could use a thermometer, but this is faster and far less clinical.

japanese mandoline

We use inexpensive plastic Japanese mandolines—Benriner is a common brand—pretty much all the time to slice vegetables, fruits, and even the frozen meat for our Beef Tartare with Sunchoke Chips (page 79). There are other types of mandolines, but most of them take up a lot more space and often don't work as well. When using a mandoline, the most important thing to keep in mind is your grip: i.e., securing the tool with one hand and having a command over the ingredient you want to slice with the other. You can use the screws on the underside of the mandoline to adjust the thickness, but to make sure the results are consistent, you need to maintain steady pressure. Do a couple of test runs first and adjust the blade and/or pressure as needed. And be sure to keep your fingers away from the blade, whether you use the guard or not. One way we avoid cuts is by wearing two latex gloves on the hand closest to the blade.

juicer

We use a centrifugal juicer from Breville (not one of the citrus juicers) to turn bunches of sorrel, cilantro, and other herbs into liquids that add a refreshing layer of flavor to a few dishes, like our classic Mussels Escabeche on Toast (page 71) and Burrata, Salsa Verde, and Charred Bread (page 82). In most cases, you'll end up with more than the recipe calls for. Juice some other vegetables or fruit while you're at it and make yourself a drink—just don't do that with the potent Green Garlic Juice (page 46), as you'll regret it. By the way, you can try to hack it with a blender, adding a few tablespoons of water and then straining through a fine-mesh sieve, but it's a pain and not always successful, and it yields much less juice.

microplane

Whenever a recipe calls for grated zest, use a regular (fine) Microplane; be careful not to get too much of the white pith to avoid bitterness. The coarser Microplane shaver—sold in many places as a chocolate shaver—is what we use for hard cheeses and *mojama*. (See Eggs with Beans, Harissa, and Mojama on page 253.)

mortar and pestle

There are all sorts of mortars out there, but I'd suggest one with a textured surface, like a Mexican *molcajete* or Japanese ceramic. When using a mortar and pestle, it's important to find the flow, starting slow before getting into it. For garlic, crush it with the side of a heavy knife before throwing it in, then add some salt to open up the flavors and allow for a smoother grind. Do not fill the mortar too high, as it will make the process more difficult than it should be, and you won't be able to get a uniform result. Also, ensure that your mortar is dry before using it.

ring mold

We use ring molds when plating many of our dishes to keep a consistent aesthetic. They also let us create a contained little environment where we can layer ingredients and thereby influence how a diner eats through a dish—i.e., the right ratio of variables and control. We use stainless steel tart rings from the French company Matfer, which you can easily purchase at places like Sur La Table or order online at matferbourgeatusa.com. The sizes we use most frequently are 3½ inches, 4 inches, and 5½ inches. But if you don't have a ring mold, just eat and enjoy.

scale

I know tablespoons and cup measurements reign supreme in the United States, but keeping a scale on hand isn't a bad idea. It's how we measure.

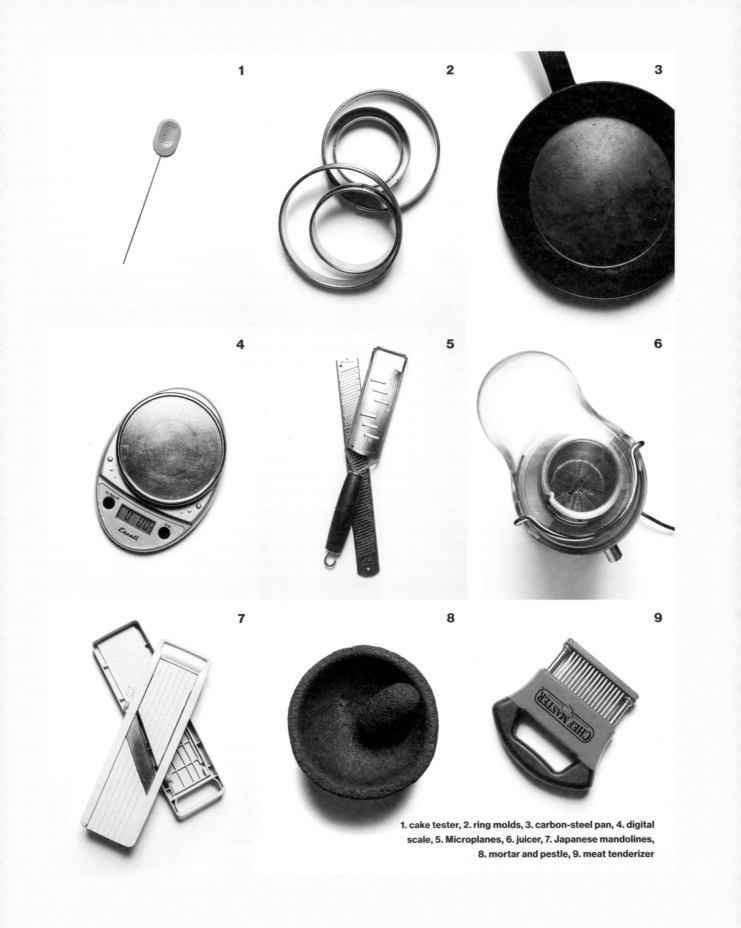

1. cake tester, 2. ring molds, 3. carbon-steel pan, 4. digital scale, 5. Microplanes, 6. juicer, 7. Japanese mandolines, 8. mortar and pestle, 9. meat tenderizer

spice grinder or coffee grinder

I recommend one of these because grinding large quantities of spices with a mortar and pestle can be difficult. If using a coffee grinder, make sure it's dedicated to spices and only spices, as you don't want your morning coffee tasting of cumin or coriander.

tenderizer

Not a romantic tool, yet it's an extremely resourceful one in that it allows you to take a piece of meat like pork shoulder, which is normally so tough that it must be braised, and turn it into something you can grill or sear.

pantry

anchovies

Canned anchovies are one of my favorite examples of what happens when you add salt to another ingredient and let time do its work. They may seem overpowering or fishy to some, but if you source the good stuff—Nassari, Don Bocarte, or Ortiz—they are tremendous. We use them in steaks, salads, pretty much everywhere.

bottarga

Most bottarga is prepared by curing mullet or tuna roe, but we came across a variety made with wild coho salmon, thanks to Jacob Tupper of Triad Fisheries in Washington State. It's sweeter than most bottarga, and it has a way of melting on your palate like a caramel. You can use it on so many dishes, like pasta, scrambled eggs, or a good toast. You'll see it in this book shaved on asparagus with béarnaise sauce (see page 118).

cheeses

I love using Italian cheeses with a lot of personality, a little rough around the edges yet unquestionably elegant and distinctive, more often meant for the table than for cooking. If possible, find a shop where you can have a conversation with the cheesemonger and taste what you are getting, since it may be necessary to figure out substitution ideas beyond the ones provided below.

- Pecorino Sardo: A nutty and fruity artisan cheese that we like to grate over ricotta dumplings. It is not as dry as you might expect from a pecorino, and you can detect a very clean and earthy essence of sheep's milk. If you can't find Pecorino Sardo, choose a Bianco Sardo or a good Pecorino Toscano that is aged for 4 or so months and has a gnarly-looking rind.

- Taleggio: I turn this very savory cow's-milk cheese into a sauce that we often pair with beef. Look for one that appears like a uniform paste and that is not terribly salty. The American cheese Grayson would be a good substitute, as would raclette.

- Ubriaco Rosso: A robust and complex cheese of multiple milk types—goat's, cow's, and sheep's—produced in a peasant style (in this case, covered in grape must for up to 6 months) that manages to be dry, spicy, salty, fatty, and sweet all at once. Testun al Barolo or any of the cheeses in the drunken style (*ubriaco*), like Ubriaco Riserva Sergio Moro and Ubriacone, would be good substitutes.

- Pecorino Duro: A sweet and nutty cheese that plays off the Ubriaco Rosso in our endive salad. It is made in the style of Parmigiano-Reggiano, in that it is placed in a brine bath for 3 weeks, making the cheese less salty than most pecorinos. The crystalline texture will also remind you of Parmigiano. Moliterno is a solid substitution, and so is, as you might suspect, Parmigiano.

- Formaggio di Fossa: Also a peasant-style cheese, with a similar texture to Ubriaco Rosso, it was originally made by aging the wheels in a pit, or *fossa*, to keep them safe from marauders in the Emilia-Romagna. Because they are aged without oxygen, you end up tasting a very clear distillation of the sheep's milk; it becomes an intense version of itself. It is excellent on salads. Pecorino di Fossa, Roccia del Piave, or a weird, artisan, cloth-bound cheddar aged at least 16 months would be good stand-ins.

- Bayley Hazen Blue: From Jasper Hill Farm, it's made from cow's milk. Balanced and decadent, it's perhaps the best American blue.

Clockwise from top left: **Ubriaco Rosso** (*top*) **and Pecorino Duro** (*bottom*); **Three Crabs fish sauce from Vietnam; crusty miche from Brooklyn**

1. Dried shrimp, 2. dried squid,
3. dried scallops, 4. dried anchovies,
5. squid ink, 6. dried mussels,
7. dried clams

citric acid

Citric acid imparts a tart taste to foods or liquids without adding a particular citrus flavor, like lemon or lime juice would. It lowers the pH of food and, therefore, is a natural preservative for things like jams. You can usually find it in the supermarket next to the canning supplies or at health food stores.

dried seafood

A mix of dried seafood that we source from Chinatown is the key to the squid ink stock for our Fried Arroz Negro (page 97). They provide a deep and particular umami. We also take the tiny dried Louisiana shrimp and grind them into a condiment that is wonderful on salads. You can source dried shrimp, scallops, mussels, and anchovies online (see Sourcing, page 296), but if you have a Chinatown where you live, definitely go there.

fish sauce

Fish sauce, the popular Southeast Asian ingredient made of fermented fish and salt, appears in many of our recipes. The idea is for it to bring the dish flavor while remaining undetectable, so be judicious, making sure your bottle only releases small drops at a time. We use the Vietnamese brands Red Boat and Three Crabs.

furikake

Among the many applications for this Japanese seasoning made from seaweed, sesame seeds, MSG, and sometimes several other ingredients is sprinkling it over rice. We like it on top of potato and egg salads. Go with a "traditional blend" or any that has fewer ingredients, mostly just the sesame and nori.

garlic and garlic oil

Supermarket garlic is often poorly stored and just as often is too old; it may even start sprouting. The flavor is too intense, and not fresh and vibrant. So try to get local garlic, a task that becomes especially easy in the spring. In any case, store it in a cool, dark, dry place. Fresh varieties will be important for our garlic oil, which we use for basting fish, seafood, and meats as they cook. See the recipe on page 46.

green garlic juice

Juiced green garlic is one of our most frequently used pantry ingredients. A drop or two, sometimes a bit more, can give an entire dish a mysterious complexity that won't overpower. As with fish sauce, you don't want to detect it. Freeze the GG juice and remove small chunks as needed, like a bouillon cube. See the full recipe on page 46.

herbs

We use some quite common herbs, like parsley, mint, and rosemary, but also some that may seem perhaps a bit adventurous, like anise hyssop, lovage, and Thai basil. Spring and summer are the best time to source all, but greenhouse herbs are available pretty much year-round.

kombu

This edible kelp comes in dried sheets. It's the basis of dashi; we use it similarly to anchor other broths, though the applications are endless.

mandarin orange olive oil

This is an *agrumato*-style olive oil, meaning that the olives are crushed together with a citrus, in this case orange. You get this aromatic and delicately flavored oil that I like on all types of fish. It's even great drizzled on top of cooked beef. In this book, you'll see it used for Marinated Olives (page 57), in a few salads, and in some raw fish preparations, like our silky cured fluke (see page 75).

miche

This is a dense, dark, round loaf of country bread that I find particularly appealing. It's great to cook with, by which I mean that you can almost treat it like a piece of meat, charring it in a pan or even basting it with broths or sauces. It will absorb the flavors without losing its structure. We also like to serve it sliced with much of our food. A very simple tip: An hour before you cook a meal, sprinkle some water on the loaf and then heat it at 375°F (190°C) for about 15 minutes, depending of course on the loaf's size. That's what we do to deepen the crust and make it feel freshly baked.

mojama

Consider mojama, air-dried tuna, a southern Spanish jerky, similar to the more widely known bottarga. In Spain, they serve mojama drizzled with oil alongside Marcona almonds as a tapa, but I especially like it shaved on all types of salads. It is already dried, but sometimes we dry it even more (as in our eggs and beans brunch dish on page 253), wrapping it in a cloth and leaving it out at room temperature for a couple of days. Another option, if you want the mojama especially dry, would be to preshave it before drying.

nuts

Buy nuts from a good shop with a brisk turnover and taste them before using. They grow rancid if poorly stored. Walnuts, hazelnuts, pistachios, and almonds are the ones we use most often. My favorite nut of all, though, may be the Marcona almond, a sweet, oily Spanish variety that you can find at good markets.

olive oil

At Estela, we look for versatile and unobtrusive varieties that we can use in almost all our cooking. These are mostly green Spanish olive oils, like Arbequina or Picual, that will not overly assert themselves.

salt

Kosher salt is my preferred salt for most seasonings—or in any case where I'd like to remove some of the moisture from an ingredient. New to you may be *sel gris*, or gray salt, a quite rocky and minerally variety that is produced in a similar fashion to the fancier *fleur de sel*, though it is coarser. I personally love its character, how it doesn't absorb the moisture of food or dissolve quickly on the palate; in many of our salads, it is a texture. That said, this is a fine point, and not having *sel gris* will not make or break a dish. Any flaky salt will do.

sea urchin roe

"Tongues" of sea urchin roe, or uni, can be purchased in trays from a good fish market. There are differences between West Coast, East Coast, and Hokkaido, but you should source based on market availability. Make sure they look shiny and appealing, and smell very fresh (if they reek of ammonia, pass them by). The tongues should be plump and not leaching out their liquid. They will keep for around 4 days in the refrigerator, but there's no reason for you to sit on uni for that long.

spices

Chile flakes, coriander seeds, fennel seeds, cumin seeds, Szechuan peppercorns, and black peppercorns are among the spices most frequently used in our kitchen. We toast some to deepen their flavors and simply grind others to use as seasonings. Buy them in small amounts, so you aren't sitting on them—the older they get, the less flavor they have. And try to buy whole spices rather than preground (except for pimentón dulce, sweet paprika) and grind them yourself as needed, so they stay potent.

thai chiles

We pickle these fresh small hot red chiles, also called bird's-eye chiles, and use the pickling liquid to bring a unique heat to salads. We have also started playing around with adding the liquid to certain desserts, like the Pineapple Sorbet with Huckleberries (page 285). You can find them in Chinatown, at specialty Thai food shops, and in some cases, even at good supermarkets. I use the red chiles as they are a little hotter and sweeter than the immature green chiles. But really you can use either.

vinegars

We use plenty of vinegar, often more than one at a time. We like Spanish brands, and you might say that we decide which to use on a particular dish by considering what type of wine varietal we would pair with the ingredients at hand: heartier vegetables or anything with a strong, deep, earthy flavor will most likely benefit from a darker vinegar, such as sherry or garnacha, which share similar caramel, toasty qualities. Sherry is usually aged longer and therefore has a more pronounced oxidized flavor, while garnacha is sweeter.

Chardonnay vinegar, which also appears throughout, has a brightness and sweetness to it that is great for fresh vegetables and delicate fish dishes. That said, there are no set rules, and you'll find random exceptions here— and, in very few cases, some cabernet vinegar, which is smooth and fruity.

Below are some favorite brands, but as I say all the time, source what you can.

- Chardonnay: Forvm or O Med
- Garnacha: Romanico
- Cabernet: Forvm or O Med
- Sherry: Solera 77

yuzu kosho

This bold, aromatic paste, made by fermenting chiles with the juice and zest of yuzu, an Asian citrus fruit, and salt, has a kick to it, and a little of it goes a long way. In Japan, you'll encounter it in hot soups or on fried dumplings or sashimi. We use it on our raw fish dishes, and it's also good in dressings, if you want to give that a try.

how to drink through this book

For so many of us, having to pick a bottle of wine can set off a wave of anxiety. Faced with a list at a restaurant or even just walking into a shop, we often feel that we have to prove ourselves to people who are there to help, or we sense the need to spend big to get our hands on a good bottle. Yet there's nothing to worry about, especially these days, when there's a growing number of wines out there that don't carry the price tag historically associated with quality—wines made by farmers who are less interested in scores and points than in offering a product that has character, reflects the place it comes from, and is anything but homogenized or industrialized.

These are the wines we gravitate toward most at Estela. They are great for this kind of cooking, since they tend to have a freshness and verve about them that matches the assertive and acidic food. These dishes not only play well with the right wine but also get better, since the wine draws out qualities that you wouldn't have noticed otherwise.

The best way to find these wines is through plenty of experimentation. You should look at the broader pursuit, if you decide to take it up, as if you're exploring music: You're going to find things you like and things you don't like. You'll gain knowledge by living it, not so much by stressing to study. To get going, it's easy to explore the subject online and order to your home, but if you have a good shop within reach, lean on them. The better they know you and your palate, the better the suggestions they can make for you. To throw in another analogy, it's like getting a haircut: You're not going to switch from place to place every time.

There are plenty of labels and buzzwords in the world of wine, but our advice would be to keep it simple and ask the shop if they carry wines by smaller production houses. Maybe mention that you have an interest in ecologically sound practices, such as biodynamic, sustainable, or "natural." Beyond that, there are a few descriptors that might help you locate wines suited to this food: lively acidity, with vibrant fruit and a good expression of minerality.

For Snacks, we'd actually point you in the direction of beer, something like an IPA. A sherry or a cocktail like a Negroni would work to start things off, too, as would a dry champagne (seeking out small, independent winemakers applies to champagne as well). Moving into Our Classics, you could explore reds and whites from multiple regions, like Corsica, Sicily, and Languedoc-Roussillon, though for the celery and kohlrabi preparations (see pages 89 and 90), one that is sharper and lighter on its feet is probably the right move. For the lamb ribs (see page 102) and ricotta dumplings (see page 93), a Beaujolais. And for the Fried Arroz Negro (page 97), any of the aforementioned but especially an oloroso sherry. For Salads, a dry Riesling, a champagne, or a crisp Albariño. The recipes in the Seafood, Raw and Cooked section are great with Muscadet, and provide an opportunity to explore wines from coastal regions like Corsica and Liguria, maybe a Sicilian white.

Mains generally call for fuller-bodied wines. You'll find plenty of great options from the Jura, Burgundy, Piedmont, and Rhône regions as well as the Canary Islands, to name a few. If you find yourself wanting a drink to accompany the Brunch recipes, a nice beer or a light Loire Valley red will do the trick; cold still water, too. To finish, we're not the biggest dessert wine fans, preferring instead an aged rum or a whiskey. But you can reach for a sweet Riesling for citrus-based desserts, a light and fresh Muscat with fruit, a Macvin du Jura or Pineau des Charentes for desserts high in dairy, or a passito for chocolate.

In the end, try to keep in mind that you are trying to find what is delicious to you, not what anyone says you should like. There's no wrong answer—within reason, of course.

Clockwise from top: **Pork with Cabbage, Wheat Berries, and Juniper Berries (page 206); Ricotta Dumplings with Mushrooms and Pecorino Sardo (page 93); Steak with Black Sesame Béarnaise and Turnips (page 223)**

suppor
players

We rely on a tight selection of sauces and condiments with multiple applications—a resourcefulness that contributes to our sense of identity. These appear first because if one night you would rather not prepare a full dish from elsewhere in the book, many of them are quick to pull off

ting

and might come in handy in your own cooking. Put the Tomato Chutney (page 42) or the Spicy Marmalade (page 38) in a sandwich, or use the Taleggio Sauce (page 37) to make a grown-up mac and cheese. I'll make more suggestions along the way.

Taleggio Sauce

Before moving to New York, I ran the kitchen at Francis Mallmann's summer restaurant Patagonia West in the Hamptons. Late at night after my shifts, I'd go to the only place in town that was open: a 7-Eleven. I'd almost always grab one of those taquitos and pump Cheez Whiz all over it. One night toward the end of the season, the clerk, who had seen me perform this ritual many times, smiled at me and said, "My friend, you really love America."

That is the inspiration for this sauce that we love on steak. It's also good on any vegetable with a snap to it, like green beans with shaved almonds. Drizzle it over fries, roasted potatoes, or a hot dog.

Makes about 2 cups

8 ounces (about 225 g) Taleggio, cold
½ cup (120 ml) heavy cream,
    plus more if needed
Kosher salt

Remove the rind from the Taleggio. Cut the cheese into ½-inch cubes and place them in a heatproof bowl.

Heat the cream in a small saucepan until it just begins to simmer, then pour it over the cheese and immediately cover the bowl with plastic wrap. As you need a good seal to trap the heat so the cheese melts, it's actually best to wrap the plastic around the bowl a few times. Let stand for 20 minutes.

Remove the plastic wrap and, using an immersion blender, blend the cheese and cream until smooth. Taste and add salt. If the sauce seems too thick, add an additional tablespoon or so of hot cream. You want it to be loose enough that you can spread it onto a plate without it clumping.

You can make this a few days ahead of time and refrigerate it. To reheat it, bring to room temperature first, then place the container in a bowl of hot tap water and stir occasionally until the sauce warms and softens; a bain-marie would be the best way of doing this. You may need to add more hot cream.

Spicy Marmalade

A variety of peppers yields an addictive, acidic, sweet, and slightly spicy marmalade that's great with steak. You can easily adjust the mix based on what you can source. It's fantastic on a cheeseburger, pork, or any kind of barbecued meat.

Char all the fresh peppers over a gas flame or on a grill, turning them so they char evenly and making sure to hit the tops of the bell peppers with the fire. You don't want the peppers to be completely black—and you don't want to burn the inner flesh—but they should be well charred, with just a bit of their color still showing. Charring peppers this way both gives them good flavor and makes them easy to peel. As the peppers are ready, transfer them to a bowl and cover the bowl tightly with plastic wrap. Make sure you have a good seal on the bowl, to trap all the steam. Let them sit until cool enough to handle, about 20 minutes. (Letting them sit in the steam also makes them easier to peel.)

Peel the peppers and remove their cores, seeds, and white inner ribs. Chop the bell peppers into ¼-inch dice and mince the green peppers. (You should have about 1½ cups red peppers and 4 teaspoons green peppers.) Combine the chopped peppers and the piquillos, and set them aside.

Remove the seeds and stems of the dried chiles, then rehydrate them by soaking them in hot water for about 15 minutes, until soft and pliable. Drain them and give them a rough chop. Then pound them into a smooth paste using a mortar and pestle; this will take a bit of time and muscle, but you should get a smooth, dark, smoky-smelling paste. Measure out 1½ teaspoons of the paste and add it to the pepper mixture.

Transfer the pepper mixture to a pot, add the vinegars and sugar, and bring to a boil, then reduce the heat to a simmer. Cook for 30 to 40 minutes, until the mixture thickens enough that when you run a heatproof spatula through it, the marmalade doesn't immediately rush back together and there's no liquid pooling at the bottom of the pot; the marmalade shouldn't be loose.

Once your marmalade is done, taste it: It should have a gentle sweetness and a pronounced acidity, and it should be pretty spicy, but not overwhelmingly so. To bring down the level of spice, add olive oil. Let cool, then refrigerate. The marmalade will keep in the refrigerator for a week or two.

Makes about 2 cups

2 large red bell peppers
1 medium jalapeño pepper
2 medium serrano peppers
3 canned or jarred piquillo peppers, drained and thinly sliced (about ¼ cup; 60 g)
2 large dried guajillo or ancho chiles
½ cup (120 ml) sherry vinegar
½ cup (120 ml) garnacha vinegar
¼ cup (50 g) sugar, plus more if needed

Preparing romesco in a mortar is the more traditional way of making it.

"Romesco"

In Catalonia, romesco – a blend of peppers, nuts, and bread – is often part of seafood preparations, and it also accompanies the prized grilled onions called *calçots* served at street fairs. Our version, used in the Fried Arroz Negro (page 97), is not a traditional one in that there is no bread or nuts, but you could easily include them to give it more body. In either case, it's good for fish, poultry, steak, and cooked alliums.

Makes 1½ cups

3 red bell peppers
4 canned piquillo peppers, drained
2 teaspoons sherry vinegar
1 small garlic clove
1 scant teaspoon pimentón dulce
1 small tomato (2 to 3 inches in diameter), peeled
½ teaspoon kosher salt
Pinch of chile flakes
1 teaspoon sugar
½ cup (120 ml) extra-virgin olive oil

Char the bell peppers over a gas flame or a grill, turning them so they char evenly and making sure to hit the tops of the peppers with the fire. You don't want the peppers to be completely black – and you don't want to burn the inner flesh – but they should be well charred, with just a bit of their color still showing. Transfer the peppers to a bowl, cover the bowl tightly with plastic wrap, and let stand until cool enough to handle. (Letting the peppers sit in the steam makes them easier to peel.)

Peel the bell peppers and remove their cores, seeds, and white inner ribs. Chop them roughly.

Transfer the bell peppers to a blender, add all the remaining ingredients except the olive oil, and blend to a smooth, uniform puree. With the blender running, slowly add the oil in a thin, steady stream until the sauce is emulsified. The sauce keeps in the refrigerator for up to a week or so.

Marjoram-Anchovy "Salsa Verde"

Marjoram and anchovy make one of my favorite combinations. Less spicy and obtrusive than its cousin oregano, marjoram has a floral quality that is a great match for the oily anchovies. This is perfect for steak (see pages 215 to 221) or roasted lamb. It looks something like chimichurri.

Using a mortar and pestle, pound the garlic with the salt until it's almost a paste. (The coarse salt helps break down the garlic.) Add the anchovies and pound to break them down and incorporate them. Stir in the marjoram, then pour over enough oil just to cover.

You could store this, but come on, make it the day of. Takes like 2 minutes.

Makes a hefty ½ cup

1½ to 2 garlic cloves, depending on how garlicky you want it
Pinch of gray salt
2 anchovy fillets
½ cup (about 15 g) coarsely chopped fresh marjoram
¼ cup (60 ml) extra-virgin olive oil

Tomato Chutney

This may remind you of ketchup, though it's chunkier and more viscous, and we're certainly not trying to compete with *the* ketchup we all know and love. It's great for roasted pork, a piece of beef, or eggs and bacon—or a bacon, egg, and cheese sandwich.

Combine everything in a pot and bring to a boil, then reduce the heat and let simmer until jammy. Depending on the juiciness of your tomatoes, this will take from 1 to 1¼ hours; keep an eye on it. To test whether your chutney is ready, put a plate in the freezer to chill while the chutney cooks, then place a spoonful on the plate and return it to the freezer for 30 seconds. Pull it out and drag your finger through the chutney, and if it leaves a trail—if the chutney doesn't run back into itself—it's ready. It will set a little bit more as it cools.

When the chutney is done, taste it; if it seems aggressively acidic, add a pinch more of sugar. You want a light sweetness to balance out the acidity of the tomatoes and vinegar. Let cool, then refrigerate.

Makes about 2 cups

1 pound (450 g) small ripe tomatoes (a mix is fine), halved or quartered, depending on size
⅓ cup (80 ml) plus 2 tablespoons sherry vinegar
⅓ cup (80 ml) plus 2 tablespoons garnacha vinegar
2 teaspoons kosher salt
Pinch of chile flakes
¾ cup (170 g) minced onion
2 teaspoons minced garlic
¼ cup (50 g) sugar, plus more if needed
Juice of 1 lemon

1. Fresno chiles, 2. garlic, 3. guajillo chiles, 4. ham scraps,
5. green garlic juice, 6. oil, 7. shallots, 8. dried shrimp,
9. shrimp paste, 10. dried scallops

"XO" Sauce

A spin on the Hong Kong condiment that results from cooking dried seafood with chile, ham, shallots, and garlic; ours may be the only one in the world that uses guajillo chiles and Ibérico ham. You'll see it in one of our razor clam dishes, but spoon some over crusty bread, and you'll thank me later.

Makes 4 cups

⅓ cup (45 g) dried scallops
Heaping ¼ cup (30 g) dried shrimp
3 small dried guajillo chiles
¾ cup (180 ml) grapeseed oil
¼ cup (60 ml) extra-virgin olive oil
2 medium shallots, cut into slivers
    (just under ½ cup)
15 garlic cloves (from 1 large or
    2 small heads), thinly sliced
⅓ cup (50 g) ham scraps (see Note)
2 small Fresno chiles, seeded and sliced
1 teaspoon shrimp paste
1 tablespoon sugar
1½ teaspoons white soy sauce
    (shiro shoyu), or to taste
¾ teaspoon Green Garlic Juice
    (page 46)

Practical Notes: For the ham scraps, ask your butcher for ends of Ibérico ham or paleta, *which is cured pork shoulder.*

For this recipe, we use white soy sauce (shiro shoyu), which is lighter and tastes less prominent than dark soy sauce.

Soak the scallops, shrimp, and guajillo chiles in three separate bowls of warm water (just to cover) for 30 minutes, or until reconstituted.

Scoop out and reserve ⅓ cup (80 ml) of the scallop soaking liquid, then drain the scallops and rub them lightly between your fingers to shred them. Drain the shrimp. Drain the chiles and roughly chop them.

Heat both oils in a large wide saucepan over medium-high heat until just smoking. Add the scallops, shrimp, shallots, garlic, and ham and cook, stirring constantly, for about 7 minutes, until everything starts to caramelize and the garlic turns golden. Add the Fresno and guajillo chiles and cook for 2 minutes, stirring to keep the ingredients on the bottom of the pot from burning. Add the shrimp paste and sugar and cook until the sauce is a deep brownish red and the scallops and shrimp are crisp, 8 to 10 minutes. Remove from the heat and let cool slightly.

Carefully add the reserved scallop soaking liquid (the oil may splatter), then slowly bring to a simmer over medium heat and cook until most of the water has evaporated.

Remove the sauce from the heat and stir in the soy sauce and green garlic juice. Taste and add more soy sauce if you think it needs it. The sauce should be well seasoned but not overly salty tasting. Let cool, then cover and refrigerate. XO sauce keeps for months in the refrigerator.

Green Garlic Juice

There are a few ingredients we use that should not be detectable. Green garlic juice is one of them: A few drops will add a layer of complexity, but unless I told you, you wouldn't know it was there. You will need only a little at a time (taste it and you'll know what I mean), so we recommend freezing the juice and then chipping off pieces as needed, almost like a bouillon cube. Defrost a piece or two at room temperature and then measure out the amount needed for a recipe, which is typically no more than a teaspoon. In your own cooking, consider using it in soups or on cooked vegetables and meats.

Using a juicer, juice the green garlic (or garlic chives). Strain through a fine-mesh sieve into a freezer container. Use whatever you need immediately and freeze the rest, or refrigerate for up to 3 days. GG juice can be frozen for up to 6 months.

Makes about 1 cup

1 bunch green garlic or garlic chives, trimmed

Garlic Oil

A handy tool for building flavor in a range of recipes, especially for lacquering proteins as they cook. Prepare it in the moment, and make sure your garlic is fresh.

Using a mortar and pestle, mash the garlic with a small pinch of salt until it turns into thin wisps. Stir in the oil. Use right away.

Makes ¼ cup; easily scaled up or down

4 garlic cloves
Kosher salt
¼ cup (60 ml) extra-virgin olive oil

Ajo Blanco

In Andalusia, *ajo blanco* is a gazpacho-like soup made of almonds, bread, and grapes. At Estela, we do a thicker version without the grapes and bread, and serve it with swordfish or sardines. It feels more like an emulsion. It's essential to get really good Marcona almonds for this, and be sure to use the freshest garlic possible.

Soak the almonds overnight. Drain and discard the water.

Combine all ingredients except the olive oil in a blender and blend until smooth. With the blender running, stream in the oil. Taste and adjust the seasoning if necessary. The sauce can be covered and refrigerated for a few days.

Makes about 3 cups

1½ cups (about 170 g) Marcona almonds
1 cup (240 ml) unsweetened almond milk
2 medium garlic cloves
1 tablespoon plus 2 teaspoons sherry vinegar, or to taste
2 teaspoons fresh lemon juice, or to taste
1½ teaspoons kosher salt, or to taste
¾ cup (180 ml) extra-virgin olive oil

Meyer Lemon Condiment

This bright and perfumy condiment, which we pair with swordfish, uses almost every part of the Meyer lemon, including the skin. It's also good with chicken and as the dressing for a simple arugula salad with Parmesan.

Makes ¾ cup

¾ cup (170 g) finely diced (⅛-inch) Meyer lemons (2 medium or 3 small lemons; it's easiest to first slice them into rounds and remove their seeds, then chop them)
1 tablespoon finely diced shallot
1 tablespoon fresh lemon juice
2 tablespoons extra-virgin olive oil
¼ teaspoon kosher salt, or to taste
Chardonnay vinegar

Mix all the ingredients together in a small bowl. Taste for salt; you may want to add up to ¼ teaspoon more. This will keep in the refrigerator for up to 2 days. If too tart, adjust with the slightly sweet chardonnay vinegar.

Chestnut Condiment

We use this savory preparation, which has a sweet, creamy finish, to complement the meatiness of monkfish (see page 189), but you should consider using it in preparations of pork, duck, or quail.

Makes about 1 cup

2 generous cups (about 225 g) chestnuts in the shell
¼ cup (60 ml) Ham Stock (page 292)
½ teaspoon fish sauce, or to taste
½ teaspoon sherry vinegar, or to taste
Extra-virgin olive oil
Kosher salt

Preheat the oven to 350°F (180°C).

Using a sharp paring knife, cut an X in the top of each chestnut, just into the flesh; this will make peeling easier. Put the chestnuts on a small baking sheet and roast for 35 minutes, or until the shells start to peel away from the chestnut flesh. Remove from the oven and let cool slightly.

While the chestnuts are still quite warm, peel them and transfer to a large mortar. Pound with the pestle until the meat is nice and chunky. Stir in the ham stock to loosen the mashed chestnuts. Add the fish sauce, sherry, and a splash of oil, then add salt to taste. Taste and add more sherry and/or fish sauce if you think it needs it. This can be kept at room temperature for several hours or refrigerated for a day or so; bring to room temperature before using. Add more stock or oil if it's dry.

Our Mayonnaise

You should absolutely make your own, despite what anyone tells you. However, contrary to some purists, I don't mind if you use an immersion blender instead of a whisk. To give you an idea of how much I like mayonnaise, I'll mention that one of my favorite snacks is a sandwich of plain, untoasted white bread with a generous amount of butter lettuce and mayo.

Makes 2 cups

1 large egg
1 large egg yolk
⅛ teaspoon kosher salt, or
    more to taste
2 tablespoons Dijon mustard
1 cup (240 ml) grapeseed oil, plus more
    if needed
Ice water (optional)

Whisk the egg, egg yolk, salt, and mustard in a medium bowl until the mixture is smooth and uniform. While whisking, begin adding the oil gradually, in small drops, making sure to incorporate each addition before you add more. If the mixture starts to get as thick as a paste, add some ice water a teaspoon at a time, whisking all the while to keep the mayonnaise from breaking, but be conservative—you don't want it to get too thin. After you've added about ½ cup (120 ml) of the oil, you can begin pouring it in a thin stream, whisking constantly and stopping every once in a while to make sure it is well incorporated.

When you've used all the oil, the mayonnaise should be thick, smooth, and a bit jiggly; if you find it too thin, whisk in some additional oil. Taste the mayonnaise, and add more salt if you need to. Cover and refrigerate. Our mayonnaise can be kept for about 4 days.

Aioli

One of the few ways to improve a mayonnaise is to add garlic, but remember that the flavor of garlic has a way of intensifying after you add it.

Makes 2 cups

3 large egg yolks
⅛ teaspoon kosher salt, or more to taste
¾ cup (180 ml) extra-virgin olive oil
¼ cup (60 ml) grapeseed oil, plus more
    as needed
Ice water (optional)
2 garlic cloves, mashed to a paste with
    a little salt

Whisk the egg yolks and salt in a medium bowl until the mixture is smooth and uniform. Combine the oils in a measuring cup and, while whisking the yolks, begin adding the oil gradually, in small drops, making sure to incorporate each addition before you add more. If the mixture starts to get as thick as a paste, add the ice water a teaspoon at a time, whisking all the while to keep the aioli from breaking, but be conservative—you don't want it to get too thin. After you've added about ½ cup (120 ml) of the oil, you can begin pouring it in a thin stream, stopping every once in a while to make sure it is well incorporated.

When you've added all the oil, the aioli should be thick, smooth, and a bit jiggly. If it's too thick for your liking, add more grapeseed oil by the teaspoon to achieve your desired consistency. Whisk in the garlic, then taste and add more salt if needed. The aioli can be kept, covered and refrigerated, for about 4 days. **PICTURED ON PAGE 51.**

"Béarnaise"

I've always referred to this as a hollandaise at the restaurant, because we use it with asparagus, a classic pairing. In truth, the exclusion of lemon juice and the addition of a strained reduction of vinegars and shallots makes it much closer to a béarnaise. So, that's what we'll call it here.

Combine the shallot and olive oil in a small saucepan, add a pinch of salt, and sweat the shallot over medium-low heat until soft but not browned, about 2 minutes. Add the vermouth and wine, increase the heat to medium, and simmer until you have ¼ cup (60 ml) of liquid, 10 to 15 minutes. Strain the liquid through a fine-mesh strainer set over a liquid measuring cup and discard the shallot.

Put the egg yolks in a plastic quart container or other tall, narrow vessel and blend with an immersion blender. With the blender running, slowly stream in the melted butter a few tablespoons at a time, blending thoroughly after each addition before adding the next, until the mixture is completely emulsified. Stream in the reduced wine mixture, blending until fully incorporated. Add the vinegar and a pinch of salt, or to taste; you want the béarnaise to be bright, with the vinegar providing a nice balance against the fat. Use as soon as possible, since it can't be reheated; if necessary, keep warm in a bain-marie.

Makes about 1½ cups

½ medium shallot, minced
2 teaspoons extra-virgin olive oil
Kosher salt
½ cup (120 ml) dry vermouth
½ cup (120 ml) white wine
2 large egg yolks
½ pound (2 sticks; 225 g) unsalted butter, melted and still warm
¼ teaspoon chardonnay vinegar

Egg Yolk "Emulsion"

A way of adding a clean layer of richness to some seafood preparations.

Whisk the egg yolks in a small bowl until smooth and totally combined. While whisking, begin adding the oil in tiny drops, making sure to incorporate each addition before adding more. Once you've added about 3 tablespoons of the oil, you can begin pouring it in a thin stream, whisking constantly and stopping every once in a while to make sure it is well incorporated. Once you've added all the oil, taste the emulsion and add salt as needed; you want it to be well seasoned but not overly salty. Use immediately.

Makes about ½ cup

3 large egg yolks
⅓ cup (80 ml) plus 1 tablespoon extra-virgin olive oil
Kosher salt

1. Aioli, 2. Béarnaise, 3. Egg Yolk Emulsion

Potato Chips

You'll likely finish these before they make it out of the kitchen. Choose the freshest, firmest potatoes. Older potatoes tend to burn due to their higher sugar content.

Pour about 3 inches of oil into a medium pot and heat to 350°F (180°C).

While the oil heats, use a mandoline to slice the potatoes into 1/16-inch-thick rounds. Put them in a colander and rinse under hot water for 5 minutes to remove some of their starch, then pat thoroughly dry with a kitchen towel.

Fry the potatoes in two batches, stirring constantly for even cooking, for 3 to 5 minutes, until they turn a light golden brown. Some will be ready before others—remove and transfer to a wire rack as they are done and immediately season well with salt. Let cool in a single layer.

These are best the same day they are made, ideally within a few hours.

Makes 2½ to 3 cups

About 8 cups (2 l) canola oil for deep-frying
4 Yukon Gold or Kennebec potatoes, scrubbed and rinsed under cold water
Kosher salt

Dried Shrimp Flakes

Chinatown is to thank for this seasoning that has a crunchy, almost jerky-like texture and deep, savory flavor. It goes with our Cherry Tomatoes and Lovage (page 165) and the Gem Lettuce with Crème Fraîche, Pickled Ramps, and Dried Shrimp (page 109). I encourage you to try it with grilled onions or in egg salad, or even on the Kohlrabi with Apple, Mint, Hazelnuts, and Formaggio di Fossa (page 90), though I would omit the cheese and hazelnuts and add cilantro and mint.

Pulse the dried shrimp in a spice grinder until you have a rough powder with a few small bits of shrimp still detectable. You may need to do this in batches to ensure even grinding. Transfer to a bowl and toss with the ground chile flakes and citric acid, then drizzle in the soy sauce, tossing to incorporate it as evenly as you can. Spread the mixture out on a plate and let dry for 30 minutes.

Taste for salt; you want the powder to taste well seasoned but not aggressively salty. Depending on the soy sauce you used, you may need to add a pinch or so of salt. Store in a tightly sealed container at room temperature. It keeps for weeks on end.

Makes about 1 cup

½ cup (50 g) dried Louisiana shrimp
½ teaspoon chile flakes, ground to a fine powder in a spice grinder or with a mortar and pestle
⅛ teaspoon citric acid
½ teaspoon soy sauce
Kosher salt (optional)

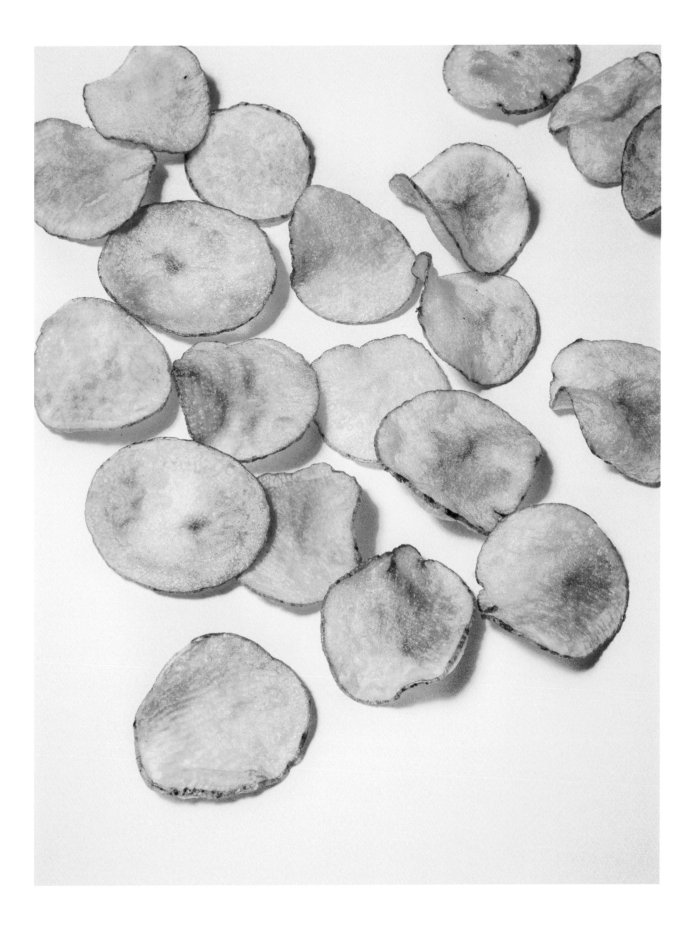

snacks

Most of our menu items require some sort of explanation from our staff, but the snacks are exactly what you'd expect: olives are olives, almonds are almonds. At home, you can pick at most of these throughout the day, and they can also buy you time if you're having guests over and need to finish up cooking.

And while I might say an egg salad is just an egg salad, there's something more to each of these recipes that makes them memorable. Whether they're better than what you're accustomed to is not for me to say.

Marinated Olives

You can find premade olive mixes everywhere, but try to make your own. Ours uses Spanish varieties of different sizes; feel free to adapt based on availability.

Makes 2 quarts

2 cups (460 g) Manzanilla olives, drained
2 cups (460 g) Gordal olives, drained
1¾ cups (400 g) Arbequina olives, drained
1¾ cups (400 g) Empeltre olives, drained
2 cups (480 ml) extra-virgin olive oil, or as needed
¼ teaspoon mandarin orange olive oil (if unavailable, go with a slightly larger piece of orange peel)
1 tablespoon coriander seeds
1 tablespoon fennel seeds
1 teaspoon chile flakes
A small piece of orange peel

Combine all the olives in a large bowl; the Arbequina and Empeltre sometimes have stems still on, so make sure you remove those before throwing them into the bowl. Add the olive and mandarin orange olive oils and mix well. The oil should just cover the olives; add more if necessary.

Toast the coriander seeds, fennel seeds, and chile flakes in a medium skillet over medium heat for a minute or so—you want them to be fragrant, but you don't want to overtoast them, or they can turn bitter. Bundle in cheesecloth and add them to the olives, drop in the orange peel, and stir well. Cover and refrigerate for at least 24 hours before serving. These will keep for several weeks in the refrigerator.

Spiced Almonds

Enjoy these with a very cold beer.

Makes 5 cups

2 teaspoons cumin seeds
1 teaspoon chile flakes
1 teaspoon brown sugar
1 tablespoon kosher salt
Pinch of citric acid
5 cups (600 g) raw almonds
4 large rosemary sprigs
2 tablespoons extra-virgin olive oil

Preheat the oven to 350°F (180°C). Toast the cumin seeds and chile flakes for 2 minutes over medium heat, or until fragrant and the seeds have darkened slightly. Finely grind, then transfer them to a small bowl, add the brown sugar, salt, and citric acid, and mix well.

Spread the almonds on a parchment-lined baking sheet and scatter the rosemary sprigs over them. Roast for 10 minutes, stirring occasionally. Remove the rosemary—it should be dried but not burnt—and set aside. Toast the almonds for 2 more minutes, or until just blond on the inside. You'll want to crack one open and check—and keep in mind that the nuts will continue to cook a bit more after you remove them from the oven.

Meanwhile, strip the rosemary needles from the sprigs and finely mince them.

Pull the almonds from the oven, transfer to a bowl, and toss with the olive oil to coat thoroughly. Then toss with the spice mixture and the rosemary. Serve at room temperature. These will keep in an airtight container at room temperature for up to a week.

Pickled Carrots

Pickling the vegetable vastly improves the classic snack of carrot sticks. We serve these with a dollop of crème fraîche and some spices, but the real reward comes from dipping a stick into the Egg Salad (page 61), getting as much on the tip of it as you possibly can.

Put the carrots in a large heatproof bowl or other container.

Make the brine:
Combine the vinegar, water, and sugar in a large saucepan and bring to a boil, stirring to dissolve the sugar. Add the bay leaf, cumin seeds, turmeric, and cinnamon stick, remove from the heat, and pour over the carrots. Let stand for an hour, or until the brine has cooled to room temperature.

Transfer the carrots, with the brine, to airtight containers and refrigerate. They should be completely submerged in brine.

Make the pickle spice:
Toast the coriander seeds, fennel seeds, and chile flakes separately in a small skillet over medium heat for about 1 minute each, just until fragrant. Then grind them all together in a spice grinder or with a mortar and pestle until you have an uneven mix: You shouldn't have a powder, but there shouldn't be whole spices either. Let cool.

Transfer the spices to a small bowl and mix in the brown sugar, salt, and citric acid.

To serve, pile a handful of carrot spears onto a plate with a dollop of crème fraîche and a big pinch of pickling spice alongside. If you're serving a lot of people, use two or more plates to make eating easier and the presentation more elegant. **PICTURED OPPOSITE AND ON PAGE 294.**

Makes about 3 quarts

2 pounds (900 g) slender, sweet carrots, peeled, cut in half, and each half sliced into 3 spears

For the Brine
5 cups (1.25 l) white vinegar
2½ cups (600 ml) water
1¼ cups (250 g) sugar
1 bay leaf
1 tablespoon cumin seeds
½ teaspoon ground turmeric
½ cinnamon stick

For the Pickle Spice (serves 2 or 3)
2 tablespoons coriander seeds
1½ teaspoons fennel seeds
Pinch of chile flakes
½ teaspoon brown sugar
1 teaspoon gray salt
Pinch of citric acid

Crème fraîche (about 2 tablespoons per serving)

Shrimp Salad with Celery

A good dip, but also perfect in a sandwich bun.

Bring a large pot of well-salted water to a boil, and set up an ice bath. Blanch the shrimp for 10 seconds, then drain and transfer to the ice bath. Once they are cool, drain and pat dry, then chop roughly into ⅛-inch dice.

Put the mayonnaise in a medium bowl and use a regular Microplane to grate the garlic into it. Add the celery and shrimp and mix gently, then add the lemon zest and a few pinches of salt. The dried shrimp will add a good bit of saltiness, so you don't want to overdo it.

Put a ring mold in the center of a plate and spoon in half the shrimp salad. Remove the ring mold and repeat on a second plate with the remaining salad. Then top each portion with a generous sprinkle of celery seeds and half the shrimp flakes. Serve the crackers alongside.

Serves 4

Kosher salt
12 ounces (350 g) baby shrimp, preferably fresh, peeled
¼ cup (60 ml) Our Mayonnaise (page 49)
1 garlic clove
2 celery stalks, peeled, shocked (refreshed) in ice water, and cut into ⅛-inch-thick slices
Grated zest of 1 large lemon
Celery seeds
¼ cup (27 g) Dried Shrimp Flakes (page 52)
Rye Crackers (page 63), or other hearty crackers, for serving

Egg Salad

The secret to our take on a New York classic is the richness of the mayo and aioli, the tanginess of the two vinegars, and the depth of the furikake and mojama (see pages 29 and 30).

Serves 4 to 6

6 large eggs
¼ cup (60 ml) plus 1 tablespoon Aioli (page 49)
1 tablespoon Our Mayonnaise (page 49)
1½ teaspoons sherry vinegar, plus more to taste
¼ teaspoon chardonnay vinegar, plus more to taste
½ teaspoon kosher salt, or to taste
Furikake
1 ounce (30 g) mojama (see Estela Essentials, page 30)
Rye Crackers (recipe follows), or other hearty crackers, for serving

Put the eggs in a medium saucepan and add enough water to cover them by a few inches. Bring to a boil and cook gently for 8 minutes.

While the eggs cook, prepare an ice bath.

Crack an egg open—the yolk should be bright yellow and cooked all the way through, not creamy. When the eggs are done, transfer them to the ice bath to cool completely.

Drain the eggs and peel and halve them. Transfer the egg yolks to a bowl and break them up with a whisk—this helps keep them light and fluffy. Cut the whites into ¼-inch pieces and add to the bowl, then add the aioli, mayonnaise, vinegars, and salt and mix until just combined. Taste and, if necessary, adjust the seasoning to your liking.

Put a ring mold in the center of a plate and spoon half the egg salad into it. Lift off the ring mold and repeat on a second plate with the remaining egg salad. Sprinkle each serving with a good pinch or two of furikake, and use a regular Microplane to grate a layer of mojama onto each one. Serve with the crackers.

If you store it, taste before serving, as you may have to adjust the acidity. **PICTURED ON PAGE 62.**

Egg Salad (page 61) and Spiced Almonds and
Marinated Olives (page 57)

Rye Crackers

Like matzoh crisps, but tastier.

Makes about 25 large crackers

1¼ cups (145 g) coarse stone-ground
    rye flour
1 cup (145 g) all-purpose flour
2½ teaspoons kosher salt
2 teaspoons sugar
½ cup (120 ml) plus 1 tablespoon
    warm water
3½ tablespoons extra-virgin olive oil
1 egg, lightly beaten with a few drops of
    water, for egg wash
Gray salt, for sprinkling

Put the flours, kosher salt, and sugar in the bowl of a stand mixer and whisk together by hand. Attach the bowl to the mixer stand and fit it with the dough hook. With the mixer on medium-low speed, stream in the water. Mix for 2 minutes, then slowly stream in the oil and mix for about 5 more minutes, until the dough comes together in a slightly sticky ball.

Turn the dough out and wrap it tightly in plastic wrap. Let it rest in the fridge for at least 30 minutes, or as long as overnight. If you rest the dough overnight, some of the oil may seep out of it; just knead it back into the dough before you roll it out.

Preheat the oven to 350°F (180°C). Line two baking sheets with parchment paper.

Cut the dough in half (we use a bench knife) and roll out one piece at a time on a floured surface with a rolling pin to an even $\frac{1}{16}$-inch thickness, or as close as you can get it; flip the dough a few times, dusting with flour each time to keep it from sticking. (You can also roll the dough out with a pasta machine.) Transfer to the parchment-lined baking sheets.

Brush the egg wash lightly over the dough (you won't use all the egg wash). Prick the dough thoroughly with a fork to keep it from puffing while it bakes, then sprinkle lightly with gray salt.

Bake for 6 minutes. Flip the dough, switch the position of the baking sheets, and bake for 6 minutes more, or until the crackers are a light golden brown, with no raw-looking spots in the middle, and the edges are crisp. Don't worry if the sheets of dough are flexible when you take them out; they crisp as they cool.

Let the crackers cool on the baking sheets, then break into irregular shapes. They can be stored in an airtight container at room temperature for up to 6 days.

Kitchen Snacks

The equations for these snacks, which sustain us at work, are pretty simple: bread + ham, bread + sea urchin, bread + anchovies. Bread + (good) ham, in particular, is so ideal that it sometimes makes me wonder why I should even bother trying to cook at all.

Ham on Miche

Wrap a slice of jamón around a slice of bread. Repeat as necessary.

Thinly sliced jamón Ibérico
Crusty slices of miche

Sea Urchin on Miche

Spread a slice of bread with a generous amount of butter, top with as much sea urchin roe as you want, and sprinkle with a little gray salt. Repeat as necessary.

Crusty slices of miche, warmed but not toasted
Unsalted butter
Sea urchin roe (uni)
Gray salt

Anchovies on Miche

Spread a slice of bread with an absurd amount of butter—as much as your heart can handle. Arrange a few anchovies on a slice of bread and top with chopped parsley, some Parmesan, and cracked black pepper. Repeat as necessary.

Unsalted butter
Crusty slices of miche, warmed but not toasted
Anchovy fillets (spicy or regular)
Chopped parsley (optional)
Coarsely grated Parmesan or pecorino
Cracked black pepper

our cla

At its heart, Estela is a neighborhood restaurant, with regulars who count on seeing at least half of the same dishes on the menu every time they come in. That's the type of place we've always liked to visit, and the kind of spot we knew we wanted to build ourselves.

ssics

Some of these recipes have been on the menu from the beginning. Others turned out to be far more popular than I imagined when I first prepared them, and people will get pissed if they're not available.

Mussels Escabeche on Toast

The lusciousness of the mussels, the tang from the vegetables, the richness of the aioli, the pops from the seeds, and much more on each crunchy piece of bread, sitting in an herbal juice. Each toast is a perfect bite, but you can use any size of bread and build it your way.

Serves 4

For the Brine
1½ teaspoons coriander seeds
1 teaspoon fennel seeds
½ teaspoon chile flakes
¼ cup (60 ml) sherry vinegar
3 tablespoons garnacha vinegar
⅓ cup (80 ml) extra-virgin olive oil
¼ cup (about 35 g) halved and thinly
   sliced carrots
¼ cup (about 35 g) finely diced fennel
¼ cup (about 35 g) finely diced onion
Half a cinnamon stick
A few strips of lemon peel

For the Mussels
50 mussels (about 2 pounds/900 g)
Extra-virgin olive oil
1 garlic clove, thinly sliced
¼ cup (60 ml) dry white wine
2 bunches of cilantro

For the Toasts
1 baguette
Extra-virgin olive oil

½ cup (120 ml) Aioli (page 49)
1 lemon
Parsley sprigs for garnish

Practical Note: You'll need to start brining the mussels at least 6 hours before you plan on serving them. Even better is the night before.

Make the brine:
Toast the coriander seeds, fennel seeds, and chile flakes in a dry skillet over medium heat for a minute or so, until fragrant. Transfer to a medium bowl and add the vinegars, olive oil, vegetables, cinnamon stick, and lemon peel.

Prepare the mussels:
Soak the mussels in cold water for 15 to 20 minutes, changing the water 3 or 4 times, until it remains clear, then drain them. Discard any mussels with open or broken shells.

Heat a thin layer of olive oil in a wide Dutch oven over medium heat. Add the sliced garlic and stir for about 30 seconds, until it just begins to soften. Add the mussels and wine and cover the pot. After 2 minutes of steaming, take off the lid and transfer the open mussels to a bowl. Continue removing mussels as they open until nearly none remain in the pot. Set the cooking liquid aside and discard any unopened mussels.

Carefully remove the mussels from their shells and remove the beards, if there are any. Drop the mussels into the brine. Add the cooled cooking liquid from the pot and bowl and stir gently. Cover and refrigerate for at least 6 hours or up to overnight.

Using a juicer, juice the cilantro and transfer 5 tablespoons of the juice to a medium bowl. Refrigerate until ready to serve. (This can be done up to a day ahead of time.)

Make the toasts:
Preheat the broiler. With a serrated knife, cut the baguette into 4 even pieces, then cut each in half lengthwise. Square off the pieces by removing most but not all of the crust from all sides. (You want the bottoms of the toasts to easily absorb the cilantro

juice, and you don't want to work very hard to bite into them.).
Slice into about sixteen 1 by 2-inch pieces. Place the pieces on
a baking sheet and lightly brush each toast with olive oil. Broil for
1 to 2 minutes, until lightly toasted. Set aside.

To serve, drain the mussels in a colander placed over a bowl. Add
1¼ cups (300 ml) of the brine to the cilantro juice and stir lightly.

Divide the toasts among four shallow bowls. Top each toast with a
generous teaspoon of aioli, followed by 2 mussels that are generally
free of chile flakes or seeds. Add a few bits of vegetables and 2 or
3 seeds to each toast. (You don't want too many seeds—they're
potent.) Give each toast a rasp of lemon zest.

Pour 5 tablespoons of the briny cilantro juice around the toasts in
each of the four bowls. Do not pour the juice over them. Garnish
with a few parsley leaves.

Cured Fluke with Sea Urchin and Yuzu Kosho

The simple act of curing fluke makes silky and elegant a fish that to me is unpleasantly chewy and watery when raw. We combine it with sea urchin, mandarin orange olive oil, grapefruit zest, and yuzu kosho, which all work to highlight the favorable change in texture.

Serves 4

¾ cup (150 g) kosher salt
¼ cup (50 g) sugar
One 6-ounce (170 g) sushi-grade fluke
   fillet
Extra-virgin olive oil
1¾ teaspoons Arbequina olive oil
1 teaspoon mandarin orange olive oil
2 ounces (60 g) sea urchin roe
   (uni; see Estela Essentials, page 30)
¼ teaspoon yuzu kosho
   (see Estela Essentials, page 31)
Rasps of white grapefruit zest
   (preferably oro blanco) or pomelo

Practical Note: You'll need to start curing the fish at least 6 hours before you plan on serving it. Even better if done a day ahead.

Combine the salt and sugar in a bowl until thoroughly incorporated. Then spread half the mixture on a plate or baking dish that's about the size of the fish fillet. Lay the fish on the mixture and cover with the remaining mix. Make sure the fish is thoroughly coated. Let cure in the refrigerator for 20 to 25 minutes.

Rinse the fish and pat it dry. Put it on a small wire rack set over a plate, or on a paper towel–lined plate, and let it dry in the refrigerator for 5 to 6 hours, until very dry and firm.

To slice the fish, first grease your knife with a bit of olive oil—just a teaspoon or so—to keep it from sticking. Slice the fillet into strips about ⅛ inch wide, then chop into irregular ⅛-inch cubes. Don't worry about being too precise.

Toss the fluke with the Arbequina and mandarin orange olive oils in a bowl, then divide the mixture into 2 portions.

Place a 3-inch ring mold in the center of a plate or shallow bowl. Take a spoonful or two of fluke and gently press it against the inside of the mold to make a little border. Spoon half the sea urchin roe into the center of the mold and gently spread ⅛ teaspoon of the yuzu kosho over the top of it. Add a few rasps of grapefruit zest, then cover it with the rest of the first portion of fluke. When you remove the ring mold, the sea urchin roe should be totally hidden. Plate the second portion, then serve.

At the restaurant, we add pickled elderberries to the mix, but as these come from a small producer in Canada and would be difficult to source at home, we give capers as an alternative, for a similar result. By the way, the sunchoke chips might be the most addictive ones you'll ever eat.

Beef Tartare with Sunchoke Chips

This is perhaps the most untouchable dish on our menu, though I should confess that it's never been beef. Well, actually, it was, until I realized that bison's leanness was better suited to a tartare. We just never adjusted the name on the menu. But bison works better, tastes better, feels better. If anyone is offended by my negligence, I take full responsibility.

Serves 4 to 6

½ pound (230 g) boneless bison, strip
    loin, or other very lean cut of steak,
    as bloody as you can find it
2 teaspoons finely diced (⅛ inch) onion

For the Sunchoke Chips
4 medium to large sunchokes, thoroughly
    washed and scrubbed
6 to 8 cups neutral oil, for deep-frying
Kosher salt

For the Tartare
Kosher salt
1 teaspoon fish sauce
Chile flakes
Espelette pepper
Rasps of lemon zest
1 teaspoon pickled elderberries or small
    capers, rinsed and roughly chopped
1 tablespoon extra-virgin olive oil
½ teaspoon cabernet vinegar
½ teaspoon fresh lemon juice
1 teaspoon well-beaten egg yolk
Toasted bread, for serving (optional)

Trim off any fat from the edges of your steak and freeze the meat in a freezer bag for at least 5 hours, until it's frozen through.

Meanwhile, soak the diced onion in cold water for 2 hours. Drain well.

Make the sunchoke chips:
Using a mandoline or a very sharp knife, slice the sunchokes into ¹⁄₁₆-inch-thick slices, so they're thin enough to curl a bit but not so thin that they feel paper-like or flimsy. You may have to break off some of the bumpy arms if they're quite large, but you can then slice those too. Soak the chips in cold water for 20 minutes, then drain and pat dry.

Heat about 4 inches of neutral oil to 300° to 325°F (150° to 165°C) in a medium pot. Fry the sunchokes, in batches, for 3 to 4 minutes, until golden brown. Drain on a paper towel–lined plate or cutting board and season with a sprinkle of salt.

Make the tartare:
Use a mandoline to slice your frozen steak into ¼-inch-thick slices, then slice those into ¼-inch-wide strips and cut them into ¼-inch cubes. Weigh out 7 ounces (1½ cups; 200 g) of steak, put it in a small bowl, and add a pinch of salt and the fish sauce. Mix together with a spoon, using the back of the spoon to gently press the steak against the sides and bottom of the bowl—you want to try to coax out a little bit of blood this way, stirring and pressing, stirring and pressing. Once the meat looks bright and vibrant and shiny, add a pinch of chile flakes, a smaller pinch of Espelette, the diced onion, about 10 rasps of the lemon zest, and the elderberries and mix to combine. Add the olive oil and mix to coat the meat, then add the vinegar and lemon juice. Be sure not to overmix the tartare; you don't want it to get creamy or cloudy. Add the egg yolk, folding it in gently. The tartare should taste bright but balanced, with no

one ingredient overpowering the others; adjust the seasoning if necessary.

Take a small handful of sunchoke chips and crush them in your hand, then scatter them over the tartare in small pieces. You want some pieces to be smaller than the steak cubes and some pieces to be bigger. Mix, if you like.

To serve, in the center of two plates or shallow bowls, divide the tartare, spreading it out with the tip of a paring knife.

1. Fish sauce, 2. pickled elderberries, 3. beef,
4. kosher salt, 5. chile flakes, 6. Espelette pepper,
7. egg yolks, 8. sunchoke chips, 9. olive oil,
10. diced onion, 11. cabernet vinegar

Burrata, "Salsa Verde," and Charred Bread

I rarely order this dish at the restaurant, maybe because reading the name I think I know what I'm going to get: some cheese and bread that might be too filling. Every time I'm at a table and someone orders it and I taste it, I am genuinely surprised.

Using a juicer, separately juice the celery, sorrel, and chives.

Combine ¼ cup of the celery juice, ¼ cup of the sorrel juice, and 1 teaspoon of the chive juice in a small bowl. Stir in the chile pickling liquid and set aside.

Pull the burrata in half, holding it over a bowl, then mix it with 2 tablespoons of the crème fraîche in the bowl, breaking up the cheese a bit. If your burrata is a little dry, mix in up to 1 tablespoon more crème fraîche.

Heat a large carbon-steel or cast-iron skillet over high heat. Add a scant 2 teaspoons olive oil to the pan, then add your bread slices and let them char for 3 or 4 minutes, pressing down on them gently with a spatula or the clean bottom of a pan. Flip once you have a good bit of black on each slice, and char on the second side. Remove your bread and quickly rub each slice with the garlic clove; ideally, the garlic clove should sizzle a bit when you do.

Trim each slice of bread so it's roughly 4 inches across, with the crust still on. Cut off each corner so you have a little less crust. Slice the bread in half.

Place your halved toasts in two shallow bowls and top each one with a thick layer of burrata that's just threatening to spill over the edges of the toast; you likely won't use the whole ball for the 2 toasts. Use a spoon to make peaks and valleys in the top of the cheese, so that it can hold some olive oil. Top each toast with a rasp of lemon zest, a drizzle of olive oil, a pinch of gray salt, and 2 sweet potato leaves (if using). Pour the green juice around the toasts, not over them, and serve.

Serves 4

1 bunch celery, trimmed and coarsely chopped
2 bunches sorrel, coarsely chopped
2 large bunches chives (about 2 ounces), coarsely chopped
2 teaspoons pickling liquid from Pickled Thai Chiles (page 295)
One 12-ounce (340 g) ball burrata
2 to 3 tablespoons crème fraîche
Extra-virgin olive oil
Two ¾-inch-thick slices miche
1 garlic clove
Rasps of lemon zest
Gray salt
4 sweet potato leaves, torn if large (optional)

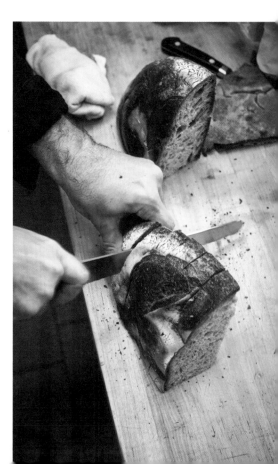

Endive Salad with Walnuts and Ubriaco Rosso

It's fun to see people's reactions to this dish. At first glance, it looks like just a pile of endive leaves. But I think there's something really beautiful about it. The way to start is by eating a few of the top leaves, little endive cups holding orange juice and oil, and then begin filling the rest of them with the absurdly delicious crouton-and-cheese mixture hidden below, sort of like making your own taco.

Serves 4 to 6

For the Vinaigrette
2 garlic cloves
4 large anchovy fillets, rinsed and
    patted dry
2 tablespoons garnacha vinegar
¼ cup (60 ml) extra-virgin olive oil
Cracked black pepper

For the Granola
1½ cups (50 g) ½-inch cubes of day-old
    sourdough (you want a few pieces with
    some dark crust)
Extra-virgin olive oil
Kosher salt
1 cup (100 g) walnuts
Freshly ground black pepper
Chile flakes
⅓ cup (40 g) irregular pieces
    (¼- to ½-inch) Ubriaco Rosso
Scant ⅓ cup (about 35 g) irregular pieces
    (¼- to ½-inch) Pecorino Duro

For the Endives
4 endives
Kosher salt
1 medium orange
1 tablespoon chardonnay vinegar
Extra-virgin olive oil

Make the vinaigrette:
Pound the garlic cloves into a paste in a mortar with the pestle. Add the anchovies and pound until everything is fairly smooth but still slightly chunky. Add the vinegar, olive oil, and cracked black pepper to taste and mix to combine. The idea is to get a broken vinaigrette with pieces of anchovy still visible.

Make the granola:
Preheat the oven to 375°F (190°C).

Put the bread cubes on a baking sheet and toss with a few teaspoons of olive oil and a pinch of salt, then spread them out. Spread the nuts out on a separate baking sheet. Toast the bread and walnuts in the oven, tossing them every few minutes. Remove the nuts once they are dark and well toasted, about 8 minutes. Remove the bread once it's dark brown and toasted all the way through, about 10 minutes.

While the nuts are still warm, put them in a mortar, add a teaspoon of olive oil, a pinch of salt, a few generous cranks of black pepper, and a pinch of chile flakes and crush them into coarse chunks with the pestle. Using the bottom of a heavy pan, crush the bread cubes into chunks between ¼ and ½ inch. (With each component, you want a mix of textures and sizes.)

Combine the croutons, walnuts, and cheeses in a medium bowl. Dress with the vinaigrette, mixing well. Let sit while you prepare the endives so the croutons get a little softer and the flavors come together.

continued

Prepare the endives:

Cut an inch off the bottom of each endive and discard. Gently peel back the leaves, continuing to trim the root as you go, until you get to the core (it's the sweetest part of the endive). Cut each core in half lengthwise, or into quarters if it's large, and toss them into the bowl.

To serve, season the endives with a generous pinch of salt. Grate the zest of the orange evenly over the top of the endives, then halve the orange and squeeze the juice over the leaves. Add the vinegar and gently toss the leaves to coat, as you don't want them to bruise.

Spread the granola mixture evenly on two plates. Arrange the endive leaves on top so that they make little cups for the dressing. Sprinkle with salt, spoon on the orange juice mixture left in the bottom of the bowl, and drizzle on a bit of olive oil.

Celery Salad with Mint and Formaggio di Fossa

Celery is one of those utilitarian, often-ignored ingredients that is essential but never the focus: Look at a ragù or a mirepoix or Harry Dean Stanton, for example. After trying this salad, though, it will become something you crave. (You might actually want to double this recipe.)

Serves 2

1 bunch celery, preferably with leaves
¼ cup (60 ml) pickling liquid from
    Pickled Thai Chiles (page 295)
3 tablespoons extra-virgin olive oil, plus
    more if needed
Heaping ½ teaspoon kosher salt
½ cup (about 15 g) loosely packed torn
    mint leaves, plus more if needed
Grated zest of 2 medium to large lemons
2 teaspoons fresh lemon juice
1 tablespoon chardonnay vinegar
A 4-ounce (115 g) chunk of Formaggio di
    Fossa or Bayley Hazen blue cheese,
    for shaving
Coarsely ground black pepper

Cut off the bottom of the celery bunch. Remove the leaves, reserving them, and separate the stalks. Rinse the leafy inner heart and the leaves and set aside. Rinse the stalks and peel their outsides lightly with a vegetable peeler. Submerge in an ice bath for 5 minutes to perk them up, remove, pat dry, and cut enough of the celery into ¼-inch slices to make 2 cups; reserve the rest of the celery for another use.

Drizzle the chile pickling liquid and olive oil onto a large serving plate.

Put the sliced celery in a bowl and toss with the salt. You want the salt to really coat the celery and open it up for the dressing. Add the mint, reserved celery leaves, lemon zest, lemon juice, and vinegar and massage into the celery—you really want the mint to impart some flavor here. If any of the mint bruises or turns brown, pick it out and replace it with fresh leaves.

Scatter the celery in an even layer over the oil and pickling liquid. If there is dressing left in the bowl, spoon it over the celery. If there are any spots on the plate that look a little dry, add a splash or two of olive oil.

Using a Microplane shaver (or the large holes of a box grater), shave the cheese over the top of the salad. You want enough cheese to cover the salad but not overwhelm it. Finish with the pepper.

Kohlrabi with Apple, Mint, Hazelnuts, and Formaggio di Fossa

Kohlrabi mimics the sweetness and, especially, the texture of apples. Aside from taking care to slice the two main ingredients evenly, there's not much to worry about here. It's going to be excellent. The best time to prepare this is late summer/early fall, when apples are crisp and kohlrabi begins to sweeten, but you can proceed with it into winter.

Preheat the oven to 325°F (165°C).

Spread the hazelnuts on a small baking sheet and toast in the oven, shaking the pan halfway through, for about 10 minutes. Don't let them get too dark. Let cool, then crush with the bottom of a heavy pan until you have some fine crumbs and some chunky bits.

Transfer the hazelnuts to a small bowl and toss with 2 tablespoons of the olive oil and a good pinch of gray salt. Set aside.

Peel and trim the kohlrabi, slice into ⅛-inch-thick slices with a knife or mandoline, then wrap in damp paper towels.

Peel the apple, then slice into ¼-inch-thick slices of varying shapes (we usually start slicing from one side, then lay the apple on the resulting flat side and continue slicing from there).

Transfer the kohlrabi and apple slices to a bowl and toss with the lemon zest, lemon juice, vinegar, and kosher salt. Taste and adjust the seasoning as needed. Add the mint and toss to combine.

Drizzle the remaining 2 tablespoons olive oil and the pickling liquid evenly onto two plates. Stack a quarter of the apples and kohlrabi over each puddle in an organic fashion; you want to layer this like a trifle. Layer a tablespoon of hazelnuts on each pile, then stack on the rest of the apples and kohlrabi, followed by the rest of the nuts.

Use a Microplane shaver (or the large holes of a box grater) to finish the salad with a good layer of the cheese. You want enough cheese to cover the salad.

Serves 4

½ cup (60 g) skinned hazelnuts
¼ cup (60 ml) extra-virgin olive oil
Gray salt
2 small kohlrabi, tennis ball sized
1 crisp vibrant, acidic apple, such as Winesap or Honeycrisp
Grated zest of 2 lemons
2 tablespoons fresh lemon juice
2 tablespoons chardonnay vinegar
1 teaspoon kosher salt, or to taste
½ cup (about 10 g) gently packed mint leaves (any larger leaves torn in half)
2 tablespoons pickling liquid from Pickled Thai Chiles (page 295)
Formaggio di Fossa, for shaving

Ricotta Dumplings with Mushrooms and Pecorino Sardo

We can talk and talk about creativity, but at the end of the day, everything comes from somewhere else. Consider these dumplings: They may look like something you'd find in outer space, but they're actually a tweak on an iconic recipe I learned to make years ago with Judy Rodgers at Zuni Café—which was actually a tweak of an idea from Elizabeth David, another one of my heroes. Judy's version was quite austere—a bare, beige serving of dumplings and carrots—but ours has something more decadent about it.

Serves 6

For the Dumplings
1½ cups (350 g) packed fresh ricotta
¾ cup (75 g) freshly grated Grana Padano
3 tablespoons all-purpose flour, plus
    more for dusting
1 teaspoon kosher salt
1 large egg

1 large leek
Scant 1 cup (230 ml) Mushroom Stock
    (page 292)
6 tablespoons (170 g) cold unsalted
    butter, cut into chunks
2 button mushrooms, roughly chopped
½ cup (50 g) finely grated Pecorino Sardo
    or Parmesan
4 large white mushrooms, stems
    removed, caps sliced into almost-
    paper-thin rounds on a mandoline

Practical Note: You will need to start draining the ricotta 3 days before making the recipe.

Drain the ricotta:
Drain your ricotta to make sure it's firm and not too wet. Line a strainer with cheesecloth and set it over a bowl. Put the ricotta in the strainer, wrap it in the cheesecloth, and weight it down with a few cans or something else that's heavy enough to put some pressure on it. Cover and refrigerate for 3 days. The result should be dense, and a soft clump of ricotta should stick to your finger when you try to take a swipe.

Make the dumplings:
When you're ready to make the dumplings, combine the Grana Padano, flour, and salt in a small bowl and whisk together with a fork; set aside. Measure out 1 cup densely packed ricotta and put it in the bowl of a stand mixer fitted with the paddle attachment (you can also use a hand mixer). Beat the ricotta on medium-low speed for 2 minutes, or until thick and creamy, almost like peanut butter. Add the egg and beat until it's fully incorporated; scrape down the sides of the bowl as necessary. Add the dry ingredients and mix well for about 5 minutes. The batter will be thick and smooth.

To form the dumplings, sift a generous amount of flour over a baking sheet. Find a large spoon—a soupspoon would be good—and set out a small bowl of water. Scoop up a spoonful of batter, level it off against the edge of the batter bowl, and then use the edge of a wet finger to slide it onto the baking sheet. (I like to move the spoon back toward me and keep my finger stationary, rather than pushing the dumpling off the spoon with my finger, because this makes for a more uniform shape.) The resulting dumpling should be somewhere between a blob and a half-moon, with a little seam from where your finger was. This will be your test dumpling. Bring a small saucepan of unsalted water to a boil. Dust the test dumpling with a little more flour, drop it into the boiling water, and cook for 3 minutes. Scoop it out and cut into it, to make sure that it holds together and is cooked through. If it is not quite cooked through, increase the timing to 3½ minutes when you cook all the dumplings. If the dumpling threatens to fall apart, add a little more flour to the batter (no more than 1 teaspoon) and shape and cook another test dumpling.

Continue forming the dumplings with the remaining batter, leaving space between the dumplings; you should have about 20 dumplings. Sift a bit more flour over the dumplings and freeze them on the baking sheet for at least 4 hours, until frozen solid. (You can make these up to 3 weeks ahead of time. Transfer them to a freezer bag once they're frozen solid and return them to the freezer.)

To make the leek juice, cut off the bottom and the rough green top of the leek and discard or reserve for another use. Using a juicer, juice the rest of the leek and measure out 3 tablespoons of the juice. Set aside.

To cook the dumplings, bring a medium pot of unsalted water to a boil. Drop in the dumplings, bring the water back to a boil, and cook the dumplings for 3½ minutes (or less, depending on your test dumpling), or until cooked through.

As the dumplings cook, heat the mushroom stock and butter in a pan, whisking to combine. Add the chopped mushrooms and simmer until just tender.

When the dumplings are ready, drain them. Add the leek juice and then the dumplings to the mushroom sauce and gently simmer everything for 30 seconds.

Divide the dumplings and sauce between two wide bowls, top with the pecorino and the sliced white mushrooms, and serve immediately.

Fried Arroz Negro with Squid and "Romesco"

An utterly complex, textural, flavorful dish whose reference points are Spanish *arroces* and Asian fried rice. The trick, among others, is the use of brown rice, a resilient grain you precook and then crisp evenly on a ripping-hot pan. The undertaking may seem daunting, but once you have the components ready—I encourage you to prepare them a day in advance—the pickup is a lot of fun.

Serves 4

1⅓ cups (250 g) short-grain brown rice
2 cups (480 ml) water
1 tablespoon squid or cuttlefish ink
Kosher salt
Extra-virgin olive oil
Grapeseed oil
2 tablespoons Sofrito (recipe follows)
3 scallions, thinly sliced
½ cup (120 ml) plus 2 tablespoons
   Squid Ink Stock (page 290)
1½ teaspoons Green Garlic Juice
   (page 46)
Scant 1 teaspoon shoyu
1½ teaspoons fish sauce
1 or 2 medium squid, cut into very
   thin slices

2½ tablespoons Aioli (page 49)
2 tablespoons Romesco (page 41)
2 tablespoons skinned hazelnuts,
   roasted and crushed
A couple of rasps of lemon zest
½ teaspoon fresh lemon juice

Practical Note: The rice needs to be refrigerated overnight.

Put the rice in a sieve and rinse it in a large bowl of cold water, draining several times until the water runs clear.

Whisk together the water, squid ink, and ½ teaspoon salt in a medium pot. Add the rice and bring to a boil, then cover the pot, reduce the heat to the lowest setting, and cook for 40 minutes, until the rice is tender and all the water is absorbed. Remove from the heat and spread the rice on a parchment-lined baking sheet to cool.

When cool, put the baking sheet in the refrigerator overnight, uncovered. This will dry out the rice so you get it as crisp as possible when you fry it.

Gather all your ingredients and have them handy near the stove. Get a carbon-steel or cast-iron pan (a 12-inch one is best, but a 10-inch one will do) ripping hot—over your stove's highest heat—for 5 minutes or until it begins to smoke. Meanwhile, combine 1 tablespoon olive oil and 3 tablespoons grapeseed oil in a small cup.

Put 1 teaspoon of the oil mixture in the pan and swirl it around, then dump the cold cooked rice into the pan and pat it down with a spatula in an even layer, like a big pancake. Dollop the sofrito on top. The rice should start to crackle immediately and smoke slightly; this means the pan is hot enough. Let the rice cook undisturbed for about 5 minutes, until it smells toasty. Lift an edge with the spatula and peek at the underside; it should be a deep golden brown, with a few charred bits.

Then use a swirling motion to rotate the rice "cake" around the pan. If the rice isn't releasing from the pan, add a touch more oil and bang the pan against the burner, or loosen it with the spatula. Let it cook for about 4 more minutes.

continued

Now comes the flip. Grabbing the handle with two hands (using pot holders, of course), shake the pan and try to flip the rice like a pancake. It's okay if not all of it flips or if it breaks into pieces, or if you have to use the spatula to turn it over.

Drizzle a little more oil around the edge of the pan, then let it cook for another 4 minutes or so. Swirl the rice cake in the pan again; it should be crunchy in parts and the pan should still be smoking hot. If the rice is not releasing, add another touch of oil. Flip it again and break it up with the spatula. Continue flipping for 20 to 30 seconds to mix the crispy bits in. Drizzle another teaspoon of oil around the edge and scatter the scallions over the rice. Leave on the heat for another minute.

At this point, the rice should be nicely crisped, well browned, and even a little blackened on the bottom; you're looking for that sweet spot between charred and burnt. There should be a few crispy clumps throughout. If you don't think it's crispy enough, let it go for another minute or so.

Add the squid ink stock, shaking the pan to incorporate it. Add the green garlic juice, shoyu, and fish sauce, scraping the bottom of the pan. Add the squid, toss with the spatula or flip to fully incorporate everything, toss once more, and turn off the heat. The rice should be salty and briny, like the ocean. Now you're ready to plate.

Set two plates side by side. Spoon half the aioli onto the center of each, spoon the romesco on top, and sprinkle with the hazelnuts.

Place a 5-inch ring mold in the center of one plate, fill it with half the rice, and smooth the surface. Lift off the ring mold and repeat on the second plate with the remaining rice. Sprinkle each cake with lemon zest and juice and serve.

Sofrito

Combine the onions and oil in a large skillet and sweat the onions over medium-low heat until translucent and softened, about 15 minutes. Add the tomatoes, with their juice, and cook, stirring occasionally, until the liquid evaporates and the mixture becomes almost a paste. Remove from the heat. Use immediately, or let cool, cover, and refrigerate for up to 5 days.

Makes ½ cup

2 onions, cut into ½-inch dice
1 tablespoon extra-virgin olive oil
½ cup (about 100 g) chopped canned tomatoes (with just a little juice)

Grilled Foie Gras in Grape Leaves

Even if you've had foie many, many times, I don't think you've quite had it like this, wrapped in leaves and "grilled," not sautéed. It might be the best you've ever tried.

First we cure 2½- to 3-ounce portions of cleaned and deveined fresh foie gras for an hour in a mixture of kosher salt, garlic, and bay leaves, which we crush together in a mortar. Then we brush off the curing mixture, rinse the foie and pat it dry, and season it again with salt. We wrap each portion in a blanched Swiss chard leaf large enough to cover most of it before wrapping it in 2 or 3 marinated grape leaves, making sure not to create double layers of grape leaves, as we want every leaf to have some char to it. Starting with the seam side down, we char the wrapped foie on all sides on the grill, about 1 minute per side; the goal is to char the leaves, not cook the foie, so a cake tester inserted into the center of the foie at the end of the process should still feel cold to the lips.

We finish the foie in a 300°F (150°C) oven for about 6 minutes, cooking it low and slow so that the fat doesn't leach out. As it cooks, we grill Swiss chard leaves (6 or so per serving, first sprayed with water and sprinkled with salt) until pleasantly wilted and charred, then dress them with a bit of sherry vinegar.

To plate, we place each portion of foie in the center of a shallow bowl and spoon chicken jus (see page 289) seasoned with white soy sauce (shiro shoyu) and ponzu (with the acidic ponzu more noticeable than the nutty white soy) around the foie. We arrange marinated charred chard on top in a casual cluster and serve.

Lamb Ribs with "Chermoula" and Honey

I never enjoyed lamb, so I wanted to challenge myself to come up with a recipe even I would fall for. I started with one of the best parts of the animal, the ribs, which have a good amount of fat and are the type of cut that people instinctively pick up and eat with their hands. To build flavor here, every step counts.

Practical Note: The brining and seasoning take time (at least 24 hours, and longer would be better), but they add layer upon layer of flavor. You could cut the marinating time in half—but I wouldn't.

See page 296 to source the lamb.

Brine the ribs:
Pour the hot water into a container large enough to hold the lamb ribs and add the kosher and pink salts, stirring to dissolve them. Let cool, then add the ribs, cover, and refrigerate overnight, ideally for 15 to 17 hours.

The next day, make the spice mixture:
Coarsely grind each spice separately using a mortar and pestle or a spice grinder. (This takes a little extra time, but grinding them together makes for an uneven, too-fine mixture.)

Take the ribs out of the brine, pat dry, and arrange them on a baking sheet so the inner side is facing up. Press on a light layer of the spice mixture. Flip them and press and pat the rest of the spice mixture onto the top of the ribs—you really want to get a good crust on there, so much that you can't really see the meat anymore. Return the ribs to the refrigerator for 12 more hours so the meat has time to take on the flavor of the spice mixture.

When you're ready to cook, preheat the oven to 300°F (150°C).

Place a wire rack on a baking sheet and pour ½ cup (about 120 ml) water into the bottom of the baking sheet to keep the ribs from drying out. Place the ribs on the rack, then cover the pan tightly with aluminum foil, crimping the edges to keep the steam from escaping. (You don't want too much contact between the ribs and the foil, but a little is okay.) Slide the ribs into the oven.

Check the ribs after 2½ hours: When they are ready, the bones at the ends of the slabs will be a little wiggly, so that you could pull

Serves 4 to 6

For the Brine
10 cups hot water
1 cup (225 g) kosher salt
1½ teaspoons pink curing salt

5 pounds (2.25 kg) Denver-cut lamb
    spareribs (cut from the breast)

For the Spice Mixture
⅓ cup (25 g) coriander seeds
⅓ cup (37 g) fennel seeds
2 tablespoons cumin seeds
1 tablespoon black peppercorns
1 clove
Heaping 1 tablespoon chile flakes
½ teaspoon ground cinnamon

For the Chermoula
2 bunches cilantro, roughly chopped
Kosher salt
2 teaspoons sherry vinegar
1 teaspoon fish sauce
1 tablespoon plus 1 teaspoon extra-virgin
    olive oil

3 tablespoons honey
3 tablespoons chardonnay vinegar
A handful of mint leaves, torn, for garnish

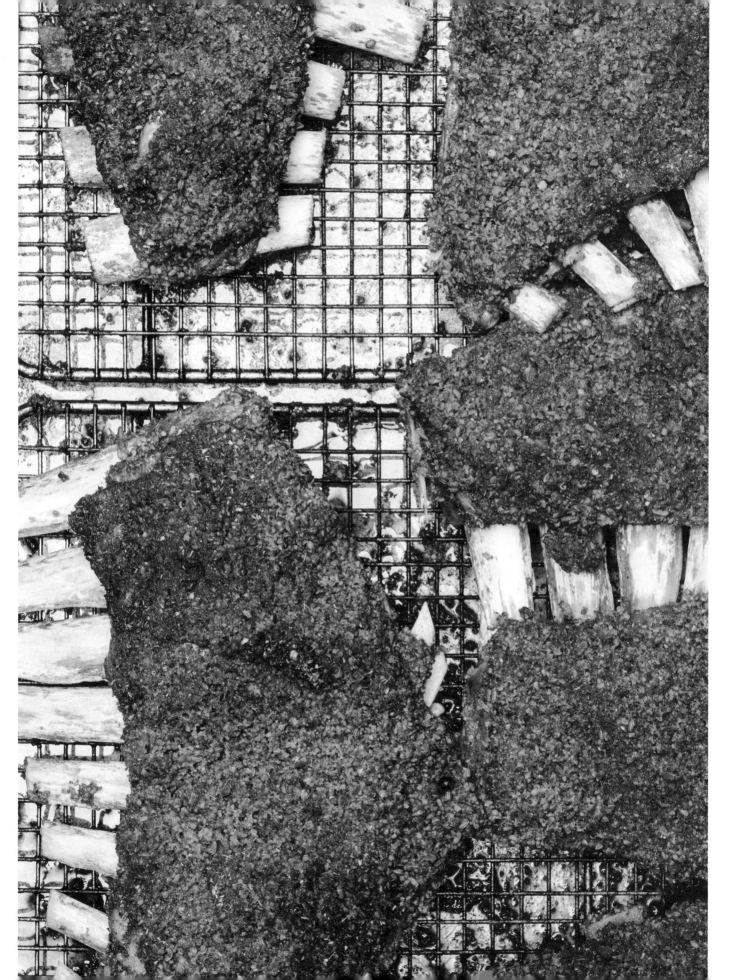

them out easily. If you need to, give them another 15 minutes or so. Remove the pan from the oven, being careful that the water doesn't spill. Uncover the ribs—be careful of the hot escaping steam—and let them cool, then cut between the bones into 2-rib sections. (The ribs can sit in the refrigerator overnight, if you like. In fact, this will make them easier to cut.)

When you're ready to serve, arrange the ribs on a baking sheet, meat side up; bring to room temperature if you've refrigerated them. Preheat the broiler.

Make the chermoula:
Put the cilantro in a large mortar, add a pinch of salt, and pound lightly with the pestle. Mix in the sherry vinegar, fish sauce, and olive oil.

Mix together the honey and chardonnay vinegar, then brush or spoon about half the mixture over the ribs and place under the broiler for 3 minutes. Lacquer on the remaining honey mixture, then place the ribs back under the broiler for another 3 minutes or so. You're just looking to add some toasty color and heat the ribs fully; you don't want to cook the meat any further. And yet, you may need to give them a bit more time.

To serve, place a spoonful of chermoula on each plate, top with mint leaves, then set as many ribs as you like on top.

salads

Our salads should make you forget that you're eating a salad, or at least remind you that if done a certain way, they are anything but a chore to eat. To avoid homogeneity, we usually dress the plate, not the salad, before building on top of that, adding one component at a time, so the dish changes as you drag its elements through disparate pockets and pools of oils and juices.

I tend to choose fruit that is a touch underripe, with some bite to it, and most important, with enough acidity. You'll note we use the liquid from pickled Thai chiles (see page 295) in many of these recipes. It's easy to make and extremely useful.

Gem Lettuce with Crème Fraîche, Pickled Ramps, and Dried Shrimp

I love Gem lettuce, a resilient leafy green that has a sweet flavor, a crisp bite, and a crumpled texture that's great for coating; creamy and dense dressings won't make it wilt. For me, though, this salad is all about the sharpness of the pickled ramps and the deep and flaky dried shrimp. It's good on its own, but it also makes a great side for roasted pork or grilled fish.

Serves 4

¼ cup (50 g) plus 2 tablespoons
    crème fraîche
2 heads Gem lettuce, separated
    into leaves, washed, and shocked
    (refreshed) in ice water for 5 minutes,
    then drained and dried with a kitchen
    towel
Kosher salt
1 tablespoon chardonnay vinegar
Grated zest of 1 lemon
1½ teaspoons fresh lemon juice
2 tablespoons chopped Pickled Ramps
    (page 295)
Gray salt
⅓ cup (50 g) Dried Shrimp Flakes
    (page 52)

Smear the crème fraîche over the inside of a large bowl. Add the lettuce leaves, along with a pinch of kosher salt, and toss to coat them, making sure there aren't any big pockets of crème fraîche lurking anywhere. Add the vinegar, lemon zest, lemon juice, and ramps and toss to thoroughly incorporate. Taste for salt; you want this to be only lightly seasoned, as the shrimp flakes will add a lot of saltiness.

Pile the lettuce naturally on two plates, then sprinkle evenly with a small pinch or so of gray salt and the shrimp flakes.

Waldorf-Style Salad of Gem Lettuce

There's a part of me that loves all these classic, tacky dishes that have fallen out of favor. We used to eat Waldorf salad back home and feel regal. In this case, there are some differences from the traditional, but it delivers just as much comfort.

Practical Note: I like using an Anjou pear here; the more common Bosc would be fine, though, as long as it's firm and green and has some crunch to it.

Put the blue cheese in the freezer.

Make the crunch:
Put the yogurt in a small bowl and stir in the lemon zest, garlic, and salt. Add the pear, celery, raisins, and pistachios and stir gently to mix. Set aside.

Prepare the salad:
Remove the floppy outer leaves of the lettuce and save them for some other use. Separate the rest of the leaves, rinse them, and shock (refresh) them in a bowl of ice water for 5 minutes. Remove from the water and gently pat dry with a kitchen towel.

Combine the yogurt, salt, lemon zest, lemon juice, and vinegar in a small bowl, then smear it over the inside of a large bowl.

Add the lettuce leaves to the bowl and toss gently to coat them evenly with the yogurt mixture. Taste the salad—it should be well seasoned and lemony, but not overpowering in either direction; add a little salt and/or lemon juice if necessary.

Pile half of the crunch onto each of two plates. Layer the lettuce leaves around them to build a little heap that completely covers the crunch. Top with a few good cranks of black pepper, then use a Microplane shaver to shave wisps of the blue cheese over each plate in a light, even layer.

I recommend that you eat this with your hands and maybe a fork, using the lettuce to scoop up the crunch.

Serves 4

A 4-ounce (115 g) chunk of Bayley Hazen
  blue cheese

For the Crunch
⅓ cup (80 ml) full-fat Greek yogurt
Grated zest of ½ lemon
Heaping ⅛ teaspoon grated garlic
¼ teaspoon kosher salt
1 Anjou pear, halved, cored, and
  cut into small rectangles, about
  ¼ inch by ¼ inch by ½ inch
1 celery stalk, peeled, shocked
  (refreshed) in ice water for 5 minutes,
  drained, and cut into ¼-inch-thick
  slices
¼ cup (22 g) golden raisins, coarsely
  chopped
⅓ cup (40 g) pistachios

For the Salad
2 heads Gem lettuce
¼ cup (60 ml) full-fat Greek yogurt
½ teaspoon kosher salt, plus more to
  taste
Grated zest of ½ lemon
1 teaspoon fresh lemon juice, plus more
  to taste
1 tablespoon cabernet vinegar
Cracked black pepper

Cherry Tomatoes with Dried Shrimp Flakes and Garlic

This is definitely my favorite salad. When the oil, vinegar, and tomato water eventually dampen the shrimp flakes, the dish ends up having an almost Thai feeling. It would complement red meat, pork, ribs, or simply prepared fish.

Serves 4

For the Tomato Water
1 cup (about 140 g) cherry tomatoes, or any meaty heirloom tomatoes, ideally bruised and/or overripe
4 medium basil leaves

For the Salad
4 teaspoons extra-virgin olive oil
2 teaspoons mandarin orange olive oil (if you don't have it, just use a total of 2 tablespoons olive oil)
2½ cups (about 450 g) firm cherry tomatoes, sliced in half from top to bottom
½ teaspoon gray salt
2 teaspoons garnacha vinegar, or 1 teaspoon sherry vinegar plus 1 teaspoon cabernet vinegar
Grated zest of 1 small lemon
12 paper-thin slices garlic (sliced lengthwise, not crosswise)
8 to 10 lovage, cilantro, parsley, or mint leaves
3 tablespoons Dried Shrimp Flakes (page 52)

Practical Note: The tomato water needs to be started 6 hours ahead. One recipe makes enough for both this salad and the one on page 114, but use it within a day.

Make the tomato water:
Pulse the cherry tomatoes in a blender or food processor until they have broken down but are still a bit chunky; you're not trying to liquefy them. Pour into a cheesecloth-lined sieve set over a bowl and tuck in the basil leaves. Let sit in the refrigerator for at least 6 hours or, ideally, overnight.

When you're ready to use the tomato water, gently squeeze the tomatoes in the cheesecloth to release the liquid into the bowl; discard the tomatoes.

Make the salad:
Dress two plates by drizzling 2 teaspoons of the olive oil, 1 teaspoon of the mandarin orange olive oil, and 1 tablespoon of the tomato water randomly over each one. Arrange the tomatoes, cut side up, on the plates and season with the gray salt. Dress with the vinegar, doing your best to get a drop or two of vinegar on each tomato half. Finish with the lemon zest, then arrange the sliced garlic evenly over the tomatoes (if you have any particularly large garlic slices, tear them in half). If you want a less garlicky salad, wait a minute or so, then remove half the garlic slices; this will give the tomatoes a lot of garlic flavor without any harsh bite.

Tear the lovage leaves into small bite-sized pieces and scatter them over the tomatoes and garlic. Finish by sprinkling the shrimp flakes evenly over both plates.

Cherry Tomatoes with Figs and Onion

I may favor underripe fruits and vegetables in most salads, but here, it's absolutely necessary to feature beautiful ripe figs, juicy, sweet, and meaty. Good with almost any fish preparation.

Practical Note: The tomato water needs to be started 6 hours ahead and should be used within a day of being prepared.

Slice ten 1-by-⅛-inch-wide strips from the onion (reserve the rest of the onion for another use). Soak in ice water for at least 30 minutes to soften the bite of the onion.

Drain the onion, transfer to another small bowl, and season with a splash of chardonnay vinegar and a pinch of kosher salt.

Dress each of two plates with 2 teaspoons of the olive oil, 1 teaspoon of the mandarin orange olive oil, 1 teaspoon of the chile pickling liquid, and 1 tablespoon of the tomato water. Arrange the tomatoes, cut side up, on the plates and season with the ½ teaspoon gray salt. Dress each plate with 1 teaspoon of the garnacha vinegar, doing your best to get a drop or two of vinegar on each tomato half. Scatter the lemon zest over the tomatoes, then arrange the sliced garlic evenly over them (if you have any particularly large garlic slices, tear them in half). If you want a less garlicky salad, wait a minute or so, then remove half the garlic slices; this will give the tomatoes a lot of garlic flavor without any harsh bite.

In a small bowl, dress the torn figs with the remaining 1 teaspoon garnacha vinegar and a pinch or so of gray salt, then arrange on the plates in a random pattern.

Serves 4

¼ Spanish onion
Chardonnay vinegar
Kosher salt
4 teaspoons extra-virgin olive oil
2 teaspoons mandarin orange olive oil (or just use a total of 2 tablespoons olive oil)
2 teaspoons pickling liquid from Pickled Thai Chiles (page 295)
2 tablespoons Tomato Water (see page 113)
2½ cups (about 450 g) firm cherry tomatoes, sliced in half from top to bottom
½ teaspoon gray salt, plus a pinch or two
1 tablespoon garnacha vinegar or 1½ teaspoons sherry vinegar plus 1½ teaspoons cabernet vinegar
Grated lemon zest
6 paper-thin slices garlic (sliced lengthwise, not crosswise)
6 black Mission figs, stems cut off, torn in half

Charred Cucumber with Ricotta, Anise Hyssop, and Basil

Charring gives the unexciting cucumber an unexpected sweetness and complexity. It concentrates flavor. When paired with some ricotta and herbs, including the licorice-y anise hyssop, it makes for a slightly unusual but inarguably luscious and comforting salad.

Serves 4

7 medium Persian cucumbers
   (6 to 7 inches long)
2 tablespoons sherry vinegar
2 tablespoons plus 2 teaspoons
   extra-virgin olive oil
1½ teaspoons Green Garlic Juice
   (page 46)
Pinch of kosher salt, or to taste
1½ teaspoons fish sauce
½ cup (100 g) fresh ricotta
8 anise hyssop or basil leaves,
   torn if large
8 basil leaves (or fewer, as desired),
   torn if large
Gray salt
Chile flakes

Roughly chop 3 of the cucumbers. Transfer to a blender and blend to a smooth puree, adding a splash of water if needed to move things along. Strain through a fine-mesh sieve into a bowl and set the juice aside. Discard the pulp.

Char the remaining 4 cucumbers over a gas flame at very high heat or on a charcoal grill, turning frequently. You want to blacken almost the entire skins, but you don't want to cook through the inner flesh. Let cool.

Use a paring knife to scrape off the blackened bits from the cucumbers. Slice the cucumbers in half, then slice the halves lengthwise into quarters, so you have spears.

Combine the vinegar, 2 teaspoons of the olive oil, the green garlic juice, kosher salt, and fish sauce in a bowl, add the cucumber spears, and set aside to marinate for 20 to 25 minutes. The cucumbers should taste well seasoned; add more salt if you think they need it.

Dress each of two plates with 1 tablespoon of the olive oil and 2 tablespoons of the cucumber juice (chill any leftover cucumber juice and drink it as a cook's treat). Arrange the marinated cucumbers in a random pattern on the plates, then dollop spoonfuls of the ricotta between them. Finish with the hyssop and basil leaves, a sprinkling of gray salt, and a pinch of chile flakes.

Asparagus with "Béarnaise" and Wild Salmon Bottarga

Look for asparagus spears that are as fresh as possible—avoid ones that are overly thick and imposing. Here they are cooked for only a moment to bring out their sweetness and preserve their bite.

Preheat the broiler. Prep the asparagus by snapping off the woody ends and trimming off their tips—save the tips for a salad or sautéing. Rinse the stalks to wash off any grit, then halve them lengthwise, if large, and cut into 2-inch lengths.

Put the asparagus on a baking sheet and toss with a pinch of salt, and then with a few drops of water and the olive oil. Broil for 2 minutes, or until the asparagus has a bit of color and is beginning to get tender but is not soft all the way through.

Put a ring mold on a plate and spread half the béarnaise evenly in it, then scatter and layer half the asparagus over it. Using a regular Microplane, shave an even layer of bottarga or mojama over the asparagus—you want enough that you can taste it but not so much that you can't see the asparagus. Lift off the ring mold and repeat on a second plate with the remaining ingredients. Serve.

Serves 4

20 medium-slim asparagus stalks
Kosher salt
1 teaspoon extra-virgin olive oil
2 generous tablespoons Béarnaise (page 50)
About 1 ounce (30 g) wild salmon or any other type of bottarga or mojama (see Estela Essentials, pages 26 and 30), for grating

Grilled Fava Beans with Bread Crumbs, Lemon, and Anchovy

There's something Zen-like about peeling fava after fava, but it feels wasteful to lose the tender, sweet husks. Fortunately, a few years ago, Isaac Flores, a cook who has worked with me since before Estela, mentioned that at his family's farm in Puebla, Mexico, they grill the whole pods and eat them topped with chile and lime. This is a small tribute to him, a nice warm salad that would be a great garnish for meat, birds, and fish.

Serves 4

2 slices sourdough bread from a loaf that
    is a couple of days old
5 tablespoons extra-virgin olive oil, plus
    more for drizzling
Kosher salt
1 pound (450 g) small young fava beans
    in the pod
2 tablespoons water
1 teaspoon flaky salt, or to taste
1 teaspoon chile flakes
1 teaspoon finely chopped rosemary
3 or 4 garlic cloves, chopped
Juice of 1 lemon
7 or 8 anchovy fillets, finely chopped

Practical Notes: Be sure to get small, fresh fava beans for this dish.

We use a sourdough loaf that is a day or so old here; if your bread is fresh, toast the slices slightly to dry them out.

Prepare a medium-hot fire in a charcoal or gas grill.

Pull the slices of bread into smaller pieces, then blitz them in a food processor into coarse crumbs.

Heat 1 tablespoon (15 ml) of the olive oil in a skillet over medium heat and toast the bread crumbs for a few minutes, stirring occasionally, until nice and toasty and golden. Sprinkle with a pinch of kosher salt, transfer to a plate, and set aside.

Put the fava beans in a large bowl and add the remaining ¼ cup (60 ml) olive oil, the water, flaky salt, chile flakes, rosemary, and garlic, tossing to coat the favas. Place them on the grill (set the bowl aside) and cook for several minutes, until charred, then flip them over and char on the other side, cooking until the pods seem about to open.

Return the favas to the bowl and dress with the lemon juice, tossing well to coat. Add the anchovies and toss to mix well. Taste and add more flaky salt if you think you need it.

Serve the favas on a plate or platter, hot or at room temperature, with an extra drizzle of olive oil and a generous sprinkle of the bread crumbs.

Fresh Apricots with Thai Basil and Fresno Chile

You may add almonds or shaved cheese to this if you want a heftier salad. It is a great accompaniment to pork, chicken, or quail.

Practical Note: You can take plenty of liberties with this recipe: Swap in figs, melons, or peaches, or add hazelnuts and shaved cheese, such as Parmigiano or Formaggio di Fossa. And if Thai basil isn't available, you can use cilantro or arugula instead.

Dress two plates with the chile pickling liquid and olive oil. Arrange the apricots on the plates and season with the gray salt, vinegar, lemon zest, and lemon juice. Place a piece of chile on each apricot quarter. Tear the basil over the plates and serve.

Serves 2 or 3

2 tablespoons pickling liquid from Pickled Thai Chiles (page 295)
2 teaspoons extra-virgin olive oil
6 slightly underripe apricots, pitted and quartered
A few big pinches of gray salt
2 teaspoons chardonnay vinegar
Grated zest of 1 lemon
2 teaspoons fresh lemon juice
Twelve ⅛-inch-wide slices Fresno chile, torn into half-moons or left whole
10 large or 20 small Thai basil leaves

Navel Oranges with White Onion and Dried Rosebuds

This is best made with the small onions you find at a farmers' market and vibrant oranges. Dull ones won't cut it. You can be flexible with this recipe. Throw in capers, olives, raisins, or even shaved mojama (see Estela Essentials, page 30) if you like, but I usually keep it simple. If you do add any of these, swap out the rosebuds for parsley leaves.

Serves 4

2 small white onions (around 2 inches in diameter), sliced into ⅛-inch-thick rounds on a mandoline
3 medium navel oranges
2 tablespoons extra-virgin olive oil
2 tablespoons pickling liquid from Pickled Thai Chiles (page 295)
Gray salt
Kosher salt
1 teaspoon chardonnay vinegar
Grated zest of 1 small lemon
½ teaspoon fresh lemon juice
2 culinary-grade dried rosebuds

Practical Note: Any bright and juicy orange would be fine if navel oranges aren't available.

Put the onions in a small bowl of ice water and let soak for about 3 hours.

Remove the peel and white pith from the oranges with a knife and slice into ¼- to ½-inch-thick rounds; you want slices of varying thickness.

To serve, dress each of two plates with 1 tablespoon each of the olive oil and chile pickling liquid. Divide the orange slices between the plates and sprinkle evenly with the gray salt.

Drain the onion slices thoroughly and gently pat dry with a kitchen towel. Toss them thoroughly with the kosher salt in a small bowl, then toss with the vinegar, lemon zest, and lemon juice. Arrange them on top of the oranges. Crush the rosebuds with your fingers and sprinkle them over the plates. Serve immediately (otherwise, the acid will start to break down the onions).

Chameh Melon, Basil, and Onions

"You've never tried this before," one of my favorite farmers, Nevia Noe, said one morning at the market as she handed me a fruit that looked like a cross between a delicata squash, a papaya, and the most outlandish cucumber. It was *chameh*, which literally means "cucumber melon" in Korean. The contrast between the sweet melon notes of the seed clusters—you eat the seeds—and the firm crunch of the rind, similar to a watermelon's, makes it perfect for a refreshing salad.

Practical Note: You can find chameh melons at many Asian markets.

Put the onion slices in a small bowl of ice water and let soak for 3 hours to remove their harsh bite. Drain and pat dry.

When you're ready to serve, halve the melon lengthwise and slice into ½-inch-thick half-moons, doing your best to keep the seeds attached to the melon; they add a lot of flavor and texture.

Dress each of two plates with half the olive oil and half the pickling liquid. Arrange the melon in overlapping rows on each plate, then dress it with the vinegar and lemon juice, making sure that each slice gets at least a drop or two of each. Sprinkle with the lemon zest and gray salt, then place 5 or 6 onion rings on each plate. Scatter the basil leaves over the top.

Serves 4

1 small onion, sliced into ½-inch-thick rounds
1 chameh melon, 7 to 8 inches long, peeled
2 teaspoons extra-virgin olive oil
2 tablespoons pickling liquid from Pickled Thai Chiles (page 295)
2 teaspoons chardonnay vinegar
2 teaspoons fresh lemon juice
Grated zest of 1 lemon
A few big pinches of gray salt
10 large basil leaves, torn in half, or 20 small leaves

Persimmon and Kohlrabi

You absolutely want Fuyu persimmons for this, preferably unripe ones that are hard as a rock and have a sweetness that won't overwhelm. (Hachiya persimmons can be eaten only when ripe or they will taste astringent.) As with most of our salads, we offer this one as a sort of break or mid-course. If you want it to be more substantial, shave some Parmesan over the top.

Serves 4

½ bunch lovage (or substitute ¾ cup/
   25 g packed celery leaves)
2 kohlrabi, about the size of tennis balls,
   trimmed and peeled
Grated zest and juice of 1 lemon
1½ tablespoons chardonnay vinegar
2 large pinches of kosher salt
3 or 4 very firm Fuyu persimmons
¼ cup (60 ml) Arbequina olive oil
¼ cup (60 ml) pickling liquid from Pickled
   Thai Chiles (page 295)
½ cup (50 g) raw pine nuts or hazelnuts,
   toasted, skinned, and slightly crushed
Gray salt

Using a juicer, juice the lovage (or celery leaves). Measure out 4 teaspoons of the juice.

Using a mandoline, slice the kohlrabi into very thin rounds. Transfer the kohlrabi to a bowl and toss with the lemon zest, lemon juice, vinegar, and kosher salt, gently massaging it as you do so. Set aside.

Trim the persimmons and peel them with a sharp vegetable peeler. Cut them into thin wedges or slices, about 10 pieces each.

To serve, drizzle 2 tablespoons each of the olive oil and pickling liquid over two plates in a random pattern. Dot the oil and vinegar with 2 teaspoons of the lovage juice per plate, then scatter some pine nuts over the top. Arrange the kohlrabi slices on the plates, tucking the persimmon wedges or slices among them. Sprinkle each salad lightly with gray salt. Top with more pine nuts.

Summer Squash with Miso and Pine Nuts

When squash are firm and crisp, and good raw, I encourage you to try this salad. The miso and pine nut mixture actually tastes like a flavorful aged cheese.

Using a juicer, juice the lovage (or celery leaves). Measure out 4 teaspoons of the juice.

Combine the miso, rice wine vinegar, and olive oil in a mortar and stir gently with a spoon to loosen the miso; you may need to add a little more vinegar and oil. Add the pine nuts and pound with the pestle until the mixture has the consistency of chunky peanut butter, with some larger pieces of nuts or even some whole nuts still visible.

Put the zucchini in a large bowl and toss together with the chardonnay vinegar, lemon zest, lemon juice, and a pinch of kosher salt. (Do not let this sit for more than a few minutes, as you want to preserve the texture of the zucchini.)

Spoon and casually smear half the pine nut mixture in scattered clusters on one of two plates, leaving a border—you don't want to see the miso under the squash. Spoon 2 teaspoons of the lovage juice into the gaps between the dollops of pine nut mixture. Arrange half the zucchini on top, as neatly or sloppily as you like, and sprinkle with a pinch or two of gray salt and a dusting of pimentón dulce. Repeat on a second plate with the remaining ingredients.

Serves 4

½ bunch lovage (or substitute ¾ cup/ 25 g packed celery leaves)
¼ cup (50 g) yellow miso
2 tablespoons rice wine vinegar, or as needed
1 tablespoon olive oil, or as needed
½ cup (50 g) pine nuts
2 green, yellow, or Romanesco zucchini, cut into ¼-inch slices
1½ tablespoons chardonnay vinegar
A few rasps of lemon zest
1 teaspoon fresh lemon juice
Kosher salt
Gray salt
Dusting of pimentón dulce

seafoo
and co

Some of our seafood might be new to you;
it might even seem unusual. I can relate:
I didn't have much access to seafood until
I left Uruguay. But now these are some of
my favorite ingredients to cook with, from
oysters to razor clams to mackerel.

d, raw
oked

The key is to source quality seafood, which, depending on your proximity to a good fishmonger, might need to be done online.

Oysters with Yuzu Kosho Mignonette

Oysters are a great way to start any evening, particularly one at home if you're having guests. Shucking can be tedious if you have a big group coming over, so it's always good to get someone to help. You could even preshuck the oysters and refrigerate them on a lined baking sheet coated with salt.

Keep it simple: This mignonette is clean, vibrant, and super easy to prepare.

Serves 4 to 6

1 tablespoon finely diced shallot
½ teaspoon yuzu kosho
   (see Estela Essentials, page 31)
¼ cup (60 ml) chardonnay vinegar
Food-grade rock salt
18 oysters

For the mignonette, stir together the shallot, yuzu kosho, and vinegar in a small bowl. Set aside.

Spread a thick layer of rock salt on a large serving platter and moisten with water until the texture of wet sand, then get to work on shucking your oysters. You'll need an oyster knife and a clean kitchen towel. Fold the towel a few times so you have a bit of padding and put it on a work surface. Lay your first oyster, cup side down, on the towel, fold the towel over the oyster, place your nondominant hand on top of that, and fold the towel back over your hand. This makes a barrier between your hand and the knife in case it slips, while giving you a good grip on the oyster. Insert your oyster knife into the narrow tip of the oyster, at the hinge, and apply pressure until you feel like you've begun to open things up. Then twist the knife back and forth horizontally to separate the top shell from the bottom, and once you do, run the knife carefully along the inside of the top shell to detach the meat. Pull off the top shell, carefully loosen the oyster from the bottom shell so it's easier to eat, and gently nestle the shell into the salt. Make sure to wipe away any dirt or wayward bits of shell. Add a small spoonful of mignonette, then open and dress the rest of your oysters and serve.

A Perfect No-Roll Crab Roll

This might be the best crab roll I've ever tasted, and it doesn't even come in a bun. At the restaurant, we serve this with a slice of miche on the side, but I wouldn't blame you if you put it in a potato roll or set it over toast.

If you don't know crab tomalley—the crab's fatty innards—this is a great introduction to an ingredient with a pleasantly grainy richness. But I won't lie: It will be a challenge to find tomalley unless you have a relationship with your fishmonger, have time to search through your local Chinatown (where they sometimes display the crabs with their innards), or learn how to disassemble a live crab.

Melt the butter in a small saucepan over medium heat and cook until it turns a nutty golden brown and smells toasty and fragrant. Take it off the heat and pour it into a small cup. As it cools, the dark bits will settle to the bottom. Transfer the brown butter to another cup, leaving the browned milk solids behind (they should be a dark auburn color).

Gently fold together the crabmeat and tomalley in a small bowl, being careful not to break them up too much. Add a few rasps of lemon zest and the brown butter and fold to incorporate.

Pour the pickling liquid and vinegar into a small shallow bowl. Add the dulse and let soften for about 30 seconds. Pick out the dulse and squeeze and shake out any excess liquid, then incorporate the dulse into the crab mixture. Discard the excess pickling liquid and vinegar.

To serve, put a ring mold in the center of a shallow bowl and spoon in half the crab mixture. Remove the ring mold and repeat in a second bowl with the remaining crab. Pour 2 tablespoons of the kombu stock around each portion. Finish with a touch of gray salt.

Serves 4

2½ tablespoons (35 g) unsalted butter
3 ounces (85 g) cooked Jonah crabmeat
2 tablespoons crab tomalley
Rasps of lemon zest
¼ cup (60 ml) pickling liquid from
  Pickled Ramps (page 295)
¼ cup (60 ml) chardonnay vinegar
6 or 7 strips dulse seaweed, preferably
  from Maine
¼ cup (60 ml) Kombu Butter Stock
  (page 290), warmed
Gray salt

Octopus with Potatoes and Pimentón

When I'd visit my aunt Ana in Galicia, she would take me to street markets where old ladies boiled octopus in pots so big they were practically cauldrons. The women would pull out the octopus—perfectly cooked, still with a bite to it—and serve it sliced, with boiled potatoes, a generous drizzle of olive oil, and a sprinkling of pimentón and sea salt.

Build flavor by brushing the boiled octopus with garlic and fish sauce and then searing it to create a crust. There's also a good amount of aioli, which makes it particularly indulgent.

Serves 4

Kosher salt
1 small octopus (about 2 pounds/900 g)
2 bay leaves, preferably fresh
2 medium Yukon Gold potatoes, scrubbed
Extra-virgin olive oil
2 tablespoons Garlic Oil (page 46)
2 teaspoons fish sauce
⅓ cup (80 ml) Aioli (page 49)
½ teaspoon pimentón dulce

Bring a large pot of salted water to a boil. Add the octopus and bay leaves and gently boil the octopus for 20 minutes.

Meanwhile, put the potatoes in a medium saucepan, cover them generously with water, and add salt until it's salty like the sea. Bring to a boil, then reduce the heat slightly and boil gently for about 20 minutes, until the potatoes are cooked through but a cake tester inserted into them meets the slightest bit of resistance. (You don't want them mashed-potato soft.) Drain the potatoes and transfer to a medium bowl. Let cool slightly, then break the potatoes into rough, irregular 1-inch chunks and lightly crush with a fork.

Transfer the octopus to a cutting board, cut off a tentacle, and taste it—it should be toothsome but not chewy. If it's not ready, throw the tentacle and the rest of the octopus back in and cook for up to 10 minutes longer, depending on your octopus. When the octopus is ready, drain it and cut off 6 or so tentacles; save the rest for tomorrow's dinner. Pat the tentacles dry.

Heat a large carbon-steel or cast-iron skillet over medium heat, then coat it with a bit of olive oil. Add the tentacles, brush with a bit of the garlic oil, and cook for 10 minutes, flipping and brushing with garlic oil every 2 minutes. After the first 5 minutes, deglaze the pan with 1 teaspoon fish sauce and continue cooking, flipping and glazing with garlic oil, until the skin crisps up, darkens, and chars in a few places. Add the remaining 1 teaspoon fish sauce in the last minute of cooking.

Remove the tentacles from the pan and cut into 1-inch-thick pieces. If any of the tentacles are particularly big, you can cut them in half. Discard (or snack on) the crispy curled ends.

continued

Mix the aioli into the potato chunks to make a chunky potato salad. Put a 6-inch ring mold in the center of a plate and arrange half the potatoes in the mold. Distribute and press the potatoes down, creating some empty space at the top of the mold to lay in the octopus. Add half the octopus. Repeat on a second plate with the rest of the potato mixture and octopus. Sprinkle each serving with 1/4 teaspoon of the pimentón and serve. (You can use a fine-mesh strainer to dust the dish with the pimentón for a more even coating. This applies anytime you want to finish with a dusting of a spice or other ingredient.)

Razor Clams and Horseradish

I find that razor clams are sweeter and friendlier in texture than regular clams, and I like how there's more to eat and more exterior to crisp up. At Estela, we prepare them similarly to the way they do in Spanish taverns, *a la plancha*. You can easily create the same effect at home, with a quick sear in a very hot pan. Here we add to them a mixture of bread crumbs, parsley juice, and horseradish.

With a butter knife, open each razor clam and scrape along the inside of each side of the shell to release the meat without completely detaching the clam (the idea is to expose as much of the flesh as possible to the hot pan when cooking the clams). Lift up the foot (the long extremity that allows the clam to burrow into sand or sediment and acts as an anchor) and cut out the dark stomach lining on the underside. Push out any dirt or sand you find. Snip the siphon located at the top of the razor clam, which looks like a set of eyes. (Dirt and sand tend to collect in that part because that's where the clam's filtering system is located.)

Put the clams in a colander and rinse under cold running water for 20 to 30 seconds to remove any remaining grit or dirt. (If you're worried that your clams are particularly sandy or dirty, you can soak them in salt water in the refrigerator for an hour or so, then drain and rinse them well.) Drain the clams and pat dry, then transfer to a bowl and refrigerate.

Pour ¼ inch of olive oil into a large carbon-steel or cast-iron skillet and heat over medium-high heat until hot. Add the bread cubes and fry, stirring occasionally, until golden brown. Drain on a paper towel–lined plate and let cool.

Crush the bread cubes with the bottom of a heavy pan, until they are the consistency of coarse panko. Season with a few pinches of chile flakes and a pinch or two of salt.

Using a juicer, juice the parsley and the sorrel separately and pour the juice into two small bowls.

Combine 2 tablespoons of the parsley juice, 1 tablespoon of the sorrel juice, the lemon juice, and 2 teaspoons olive oil in a small bowl and mix well. Set aside.

continued

Serves 4

20 razor clams
    (1 to 1½ pounds; 450 to 675 g)
Extra-virgin olive oil
¼ baguette, cut into ½-inch cubes
Chile flakes
Kosher salt
1 bunch parsley
1 bunch sorrel
½ teaspoon fresh lemon juice
½ cup (120 ml) Garlic Oil (page 46)
A 2-inch piece of fresh horseradish,
    peeled
A few rasps of lemon zest

Seafood, Raw and Cooked

Season each clam with a pinch of salt and a good spoonful of the garlic oil. Heat a large carbon-steel or cast-iron skillet over medium-high heat until very hot (you will need to cook the clams in two batches—or use two pans, if you have them). Add a touch of olive oil to the pan, increase the heat to high, and then add the clams, flesh side down. Cook the clams, pressing down on them so they don't seize up and close, for 2 to 3 minutes, until they brown lightly.

Add a little olive oil to the pan to help release the clams and arrange the clams on four plates. Dress each one with a few drops of the green juice and a small spoonful of the bread crumbs. Shave a generous layer of horseradish over each plate using a Microplane shaver, add a few rasps of lemon zest, and serve.

Razor Clams with "XO" Sauce

This take on razor clams incorporates our version of XO sauce, a robust and habit-forming condiment that includes dried seafood, chile peppers, and onions.

Serves 4

20 razor clams
   (1 to 1½ pounds; 450 to 675 g)
2 bunches parsley
1 bunch sorrel
Kosher salt
Garlic Oil (page 46)
Extra-virgin olive oil
½ cup (120 ml) XO Sauce (page 45)
Good olive oil, for drizzling

With a butter knife, open each razor clam and scrape along the inside of each side of the shell to release the meat without completely detaching the clam (the idea is to expose as much of the flesh as possible to the hot pan when cooking the clams). Lift up the foot (the long extremity that allows the clam to burrow into sand or sediment and acts as an anchor) and cut out the dark stomach lining on the underside. Push out any dirt or sand you find. Snip the siphon located at the top of the razor clam, which looks like a set of eyes. (Dirt and sand tend to collect in that part because that's where the clam's filtering system is located.)

Put the clams in a colander and rinse under cold running water for 20 to 30 seconds to remove any remaining grit or dirt. (If you're worried that your clams are particularly sandy or dirty, you can soak them in salt water in the refrigerator for an hour or so, then drain and rinse well.) Drain the clams and pat dry, then transfer to a bowl and refrigerate.

Using a juicer, juice the parsley and sorrel separately and pour the juice into two small bowls.

Combine ¼ cup (60 ml) each of the parsley and the sorrel juice in another small bowl. Set aside.

Season each clam with a pinch of salt and a good spoonful of the garlic oil. Heat a large carbon-steel or cast-iron skillet over medium-high heat until very hot (you will need to cook the clams in two batches—or use two pans, if you have them). Add a touch of olive oil to the pan, increase the heat to high, and add the clams, flesh side down. Cook the clams, pressing down on them so they don't seize up and close, for 2 to 3 minutes, until lightly browned.

Add a little olive oil to the pan to help release the clams and distribute the clams on four plates. Top each serving with a tablespoon or so of the XO sauce, then drizzle generously with good olive oil. Pour the green juice over the clams and serve.

Scallops with Peas, Lardo, and Collard Greens

This one will always be dear to me, thanks to the satiny greens cooked in lardo, the pop of the fresh peas, and the caramelized surface of the scallops—everything barely cooked. It feels grown-up and just right. Make sure the scallops are dry so they sear well.

Serves 4

6 large scallops (see Note), patted dry
Kosher salt
Extra-virgin olive oil
½ cup (about 100 g) cubed (¼-inch) lardo
2 tablespoons lard
1 cup shelled fresh peas (see Note)
3 collard leaves, torn into roughly
   2 by 3-inch pieces
½ lemon

Practical Notes: We use U-10 scallops here; the size designation means there are only 10 of these large scallops per pound. Just grab the biggest ones you can find.

Get the freshest and most tender peas possible.

Heat a large carbon-steel or cast-iron skillet over medium-high heat until hot. Salt both sides of the scallops, then place them in the dry pan, pressing down on them with a spatula so they develop a good crust. Cook for 2 minutes, or until browned on the first side, then add a thin spill of olive oil, carefully flip the scallops, and cook for 20 to 30 seconds on the other side; the scallops should be just barely cooked through. Transfer to a plate.

Warm the lardo and lard (one is cured, the other is not) in a small saucepan over medium-low heat for about 30 seconds, until the lardo begins to turn translucent and the edges soften. Add the peas and a splash of water to help them cook and cook just until the peas are bright green, about 2 minutes. Add the collard leaves and cook until they wilt, then season with a pinch of salt and remove from the heat.

Remove the collard leaves from the peas and place a spoonful of the peas and lardo on each of four plates. Top with the scallops, season with a squeeze of lemon juice, then top with the collards and serve.

Raw Scallops with Green Tomatoes and Basil

In a funny way, this both looks and eats like a bright, oceanic Caprese salad. Is it better? That's up to you, but I happen to think so.

To brine the scallops, combine the water and kosher salt in a small nonreactive container, stirring to dissolve the salt. Add the scallops and refrigerate for 20 minutes.

Drain the scallops and pat dry. Put them on a paper towel–lined plate and refrigerate for 20 minutes.

Slice the scallops into ¼-inch-thick rounds: Lay a scallop on one flat side and slice into coins in one smooth movement for each cut, starting near the heel of the knife. You should get 5 or 6 slices per scallop. Repeat with the remaining scallops.

Arrange the scallop slices on a large plate or baking sheet and sprinkle each one lightly with gray salt. Smear a tiny amount of yuzu kosho onto each slice.

To serve, drizzle half the pickling liquid, olive oil, and mandarin orange olive oil over the center of a plate, then arrange half the scallop slices on top in a circular shape, overlapping the slices. Repeat on a second plate with the remaining pickling liquid, oils, and scallops.

If you have them, break up 3 or 4 basil buds and scatter them over the scallops. Tear the basil leaves into tiny pieces and lay those atop the scallops. Grate 4 or 5 rasps of lemon over each plate. Finish each one with about 10 green tomato slices, arranging them so they overlap a bit and cover the scallops completely. If the tomatoes aren't very acidic, dress them with a tiny amount of vinegar.

Serves 4

4 cups (scant 1 l) water
¾ cup (150 g) kosher salt
6 large scallops (preferably U-10;
**   see Notes, page 149)**
Gray salt
⅛ teaspoon yuzu kosho
**   (see Estela Essentials, page 31)**
About 2½ teaspoons pickling liquid
**   from Pickled Thai Chiles (page 295)**
About 2 teaspoons Arbequina olive oil
¼ teaspoon mandarin orange olive oil
A few basil buds if you can find them, or
**   3 basil leaves**
1 lemon
2 firm green tomatoes, sliced into
**   ⅛-inch-thick rounds**
Chardonnay vinegar (optional)

Cured Fluke with Kohlrabi and Avocado

Not too many of our dishes have a Mexican feel, but this one, which we serve in late summer, is an exception. The smashed avocado and slivers of serrano peppers give off the vibe, but so does the kohlrabi, which has something in common with jicama.

Serves 4

¾ cup (150 g) kosher salt, plus a
   couple of pinches
¼ cup (50 g) sugar
One 6-ounce (170 g) fluke fillet
Olive oil
1 ripe avocado
1 teaspoon fresh lemon juice
1 small kohlrabi (green or purple)
2 teaspoons yuzu juice
   (or substitute fresh lemon juice)
2 teaspoons chardonnay vinegar
¼ teaspoon yuzu kosho
   (see Estela Essentials, page 31)
1 serrano pepper, sliced into coins
Rasps of white grapefruit zest
   (preferably oro blanco) or pomelo
2 teaspoons white grapefruit juice
½ teaspoon mandarin orange olive oil
Gray salt

Practical Note: You'll need to start curing the fish at least 6 hours before serving it. You can even cure it a day ahead, if that's easier.

Combine the ¾ cup salt and the sugar in a bowl until thoroughly incorporated. Then spread half the mixture on a plate or baking dish that's about the size of the fish fillet. Lay the fish on the mixture and cover with the remaining mix. Make sure the fish is thoroughly coated. Let cure in the refrigerator for 20 to 25 minutes.

Rinse the fish and pat dry. Put it on a paper towel–lined plate and refrigerate, uncovered, for 5 to 6 hours, until very dry and firm.

To slice your fish, first grease your knife with a bit of olive oil—just a teaspoon or so—to keep it from sticking. Cut the fillet into slices about ¼ inch wide, then slice these into 2-inch lengths.

Halve, pit, and peel the avocado. Transfer the flesh to a bowl and mash with a fork until you have a smooth paste. Add the lemon juice and a good pinch of kosher salt. Set aside.

Cut off the top and bottom of the kohlrabi, then peel it with a sharp paring knife, removing the waxy outer skin and the beige flesh just underneath it. Using a mandoline, slice it into 1/16-inch-thick rounds. It should be slightly translucent, with only a bit of crunch. Transfer to a bowl and dress with the yuzu juice, vinegar, and a pinch of kosher salt.

To serve, spoon a tablespoon of the avocado mixture in a small circle in the center of each of four plates. Cover each one with about 10 strips of fluke, then dab each strip with a tiny bit of yuzu kosho. Top each with a slice of serrano. Dress each one with a few rasps of grapefruit zest, a scant teaspoon of grapefruit juice, a few drops of the mandarin orange olive oil, and a tiny sprinkle of gray salt. Cover with the kohlrabi circles in an attempt to hide everything else. Serve immediately.

Cured Fluke with Green Beans and Avocado

This is best in summer when you can get crisp and juicy green beans.

Serves 4

¾ cup (150 g) kosher salt, plus a couple
    of pinches
¼ cup (50 g) sugar
One 6-ounce (170 g) fluke fillet
Extra-virgin olive oil
1½ teaspoons Arbequina olive oil
1 teaspoon mandarin orange olive oil
6 green beans, cut into ⅛-inch-wide coins
1 teaspoon chardonnay vinegar
1 teaspoon yuzu juice (or substitute fresh
    lemon juice)
½ avocado
½ teaspoon fresh lemon juice
¼ teaspoon yuzu kosho (see Estela
    Essentials, page 31)
Rasps of white grapefruit zest (preferably
    oro blanco) or pomelo
1 tablespoon white grapefruit juice

Practical Note: You'll need to start curing the fish at least 7 hours before serving it. You can even cure it a day ahead, if that is easier.

Combine the ¾ cup salt and the sugar in a bowl until thoroughly incorporated. Then spread half the mixture on a plate or baking dish that's about the size of the fish fillet. Lay the fish on the mixture and cover with the remaining mix. Make sure the fish is thoroughly coated. Let cure in the refrigerator for 20 to 25 minutes.

Rinse the fish off and pat dry. Put it on a paper towel–lined plate and refrigerate, uncovered, for 5 to 6 hours, until very dry and firm.

To chop your fish, first grease your knife with a bit of olive oil—just a teaspoon or so—to keep it from sticking. Slice the fluke into strips about ¼ inch wide, then roughly chop into ¼- to ⅛-inch cubes; don't worry about being too precise. Transfer the fluke to a small bowl and mix with the Arbequina and mandarin orange olive oils, gently massaging the oils into the fish with the back of a spoon.

Put the chopped beans in another small bowl and season with the vinegar, yuzu juice, and a pinch of salt.

Put the avocado in a small bowl and mash with a fork until you have a smooth paste. Add a pinch of salt and the lemon juice.

Put a 3¼-inch ring mold in the center of a serving plate and spread half the avocado in the mold, leaving a bit of a border all around. Layer on half the sliced beans and then half the fluke, gently pressing the fluke down to cover everything. Spread it with ⅛ teaspoon of the yuzu kosho. Remove the ring mold and repeat on a second plate with the remaining avocado, beans, fluke, and yuzu kosho. Dress each plate with a few rasps of grapefruit zest, half the grapefruit juice, and a few drops of olive oil.

Omelet with Sea Urchin and Crème Fraîche

Seeing an omelet on an American menu at any other time than breakfast may invite suspicion, but not for me. This is an homage to Elizabeth David's *An Omelette and a Glass of Wine*.

Whisk the eggs and kosher salt together with a fork in a small bowl so that the yolks and whites are thoroughly combined.

Heat the butter in a large nonstick skillet over medium heat. Once the butter melts completely and becomes foamy, add the eggs. As soon as they hit the pan, begin stirring them constantly with a heatproof spatula in a gentle circular motion. The key is to agitate the eggs over the entire surface so you don't overcook it in certain spots. Use your other hand to tip and swirl the pan, allowing the uncooked egg to flow under the cooked egg and hit the hot surface. Periodically scrape down the sides of the pan to keep the edges of the omelet from drying out.

Once you have a good layer of set eggs, after about 30 seconds, stop stirring, turn off the heat, and let the heat of the pan continue to cook the eggs. When there's just a thin slick of runny egg on top, add a line of the sea urchin roe just off center. Fold the narrower half of the omelet over it, then fold that over itself in the pan.

Fold the omelet over the last bit of itself as you roll it gently out of the pan onto the plate (a plastic dough scraper can be helpful here). Add a dollop of crème fraîche on the side of the plate. Finish with a sprinkle of gray salt.

Serves 1 or 2

2 large eggs
⅛ teaspoon kosher salt
1½ tablespoons (21 g) unsalted butter, cut into a few pieces
3 pieces sea urchin roe (uni; see Estela Essentials, page 30)
Crème fraîche
Gray salt

Sardines and Mackerel

Sardines and mackerel are rich, oily, delicious, healthy, sustainable—and well suited to assertive seasonings and garnishes. Keep in mind that they have a short shelf life, so sourcing them fresh is key. They're also fun to grill over quality charcoal or wood, should you be so inclined.

Sardines with Kale, Pine Nuts, and Raisins

Creamy kale, raisins soaked in vinegar, and a juicy sardine. This could be a nice appetizer, but feel free to double, triple, or quadruple the recipe based on your appetite.

Rinse the sardines and pat dry, then transfer to a plate and let them come to room temperature while you prepare the salad.

Put the kale in a bowl and pour over the ajo blanco. Massage the sauce into the kale for a minute or so, until it softens and becomes more pleasant to eat. Try a bite, and add a pinch of kosher salt if necessary.

Roughly chop the pine nuts—just run your knife through them once or twice—and set aside. Soak the raisins in the chardonnay vinegar and warm water in a small cup.

Give your sardines a good pinch of kosher salt on each side, as well as inside. Coat them with the garlic oil, then give the whole plate of them a pinch or two of chile flakes.

Heat a large carbon-steel or cast-iron skillet over medium-high heat until hot. Add a tablespoon or two of olive oil, enough that you have a good layer of it so the fish won't stick, and heat it. Add the sardines and cook for 1½ minutes. Flip them carefully, with a fish spatula if you have one, and cook until their flesh becomes opaque, another 1½ minutes or so. Just before you remove the fish, splash them with the sherry vinegar and fish sauce, both for flavor and to help release the skin from the pan.

Drain the raisins. Place 2 or 3 fish on each plate and arrange a pile of kale, topped with a sprinkle of the pine nuts and raisins, next to them. Finish the greens with a pinch of flaky salt and serve.

Serves 4

8 to 12 fresh sardines (5 to 6 inches long), scaled and gutted
5 leaves curly kale, washed, stemmed, and torn into large bite-sized pieces
⅓ cup (80 ml) Ajo Blanco (page 46)
Kosher salt
3 tablespoons pine nuts
2 tablespoons golden raisins
1½ teaspoons chardonnay vinegar
1 tablespoon warm water
2 tablespoons Garlic Oil (page 46)
Chile flakes
Extra-virgin olive oil
Sherry vinegar
Fish sauce
Flaky salt

Boston Mackerel with Grapes and Lardo

Get some good grapes and see what happens when you cook them in pig's fat. The crust (here and on page 165) is strong and aromatic, balancing the richness of the fish.

Serves 4

4 whole mackerel, gutted and cleaned
1 tablespoon green peppercorns
1 tablespoon coriander seeds
2 tablespoons Garlic Oil (page 46)
Scant 2 teaspoons kosher salt, plus
     a pinch
1½ tablespoons extra-virgin olive oil, or
     as needed
1 tablespoon fish sauce
½ cup (about 100 g) cubed (¼-inch) lardo
1 tablespoon lard
1 cup (150 g) thin-skinned light-colored
     seedless grapes
4 teaspoons sherry vinegar

Practical Note: We like Bronx grapes, sometimes described as a cross between Concord and Thompson seedless, but they can be tough to find, so simply use the best grapes you can get.

Remove the mackerel from the refrigerator about an hour before you plan on cooking it and let it come to room temperature.

Grind the peppercorns and then the coriander seeds in a spice grinder or using a mortar and pestle until finely ground but not a powder.

When the mackerel has warmed to room temperature, brush each fish on both sides with some of the garlic oil. Sprinkle generously on both sides with the salt, then pat on the spices to make a crust. Set aside.

Heat a large carbon-steel or cast-iron skillet over medium-high heat. Once it's good and hot, add the olive oil, then add the fish. If you need to cook the fish in two batches, you can keep the first batch warm in a 200°F (95°C) oven on a wire rack set atop a baking sheet, then give it a quick go in the pan again before serving. Cook for 2 minutes, or until golden brown on the first side, then flip and cook for 2 to 3 more minutes, until the fish has a nice golden brown crust on the second side. A cake tester inserted into the thickest part of a fish should feel warm when pressed to your lip. Just before you remove the fish, splash it with the fish sauce, both for flavor and to help release the crispy skin from the pan.

Warm the lardo and lard in a small saucepan over medium-low heat for 30 seconds to 1 minute, until the lardo begins to turn translucent and the edges soften. Add the grapes and cook, stirring, until they begin to burst, about 2 minutes. Season with a pinch of salt and turn off the heat.

Arrange the fish on four plates and dress with the vinegar. Place a pile of grapes next to each fish and serve.

Boston Mackerel with Cherry Tomatoes and Lovage

A perfect summer dish that features one of my favorite herbs, lovage, which tastes like a burst of celery. If you can't find fresh lovage, or simply don't like it—some people *hate* it—cilantro would be fine. I'd suggest some potato salad on the side.

Serves 4

4 whole mackerel, gutted and cleaned
1 tablespoon green peppercorns
1 tablespoon coriander seeds
2 tablespoons Garlic Oil (page 46)
Scant 2 teaspoons kosher salt, plus more
  as needed
20 to 24 cherry tomatoes, quartered
2 garlic cloves, very thinly sliced
1 shallot, sliced ⅛ inch thick and soaked
  in ice water for 1 hour
½ teaspoon chardonnay vinegar
½ teaspoon garnacha vinegar
4 basil leaves
4 lovage leaves
1½ tablespoons extra-virgin olive oil, or
  as needed
1 tablespoon fish sauce
4 teaspoons sherry vinegar

Remove the mackerel from the refrigerator about an hour before you plan on cooking it and let it come to room temperature.

Grind the peppercorns and then the coriander seeds in a spice grinder or with a mortar and pestle until finely ground but not a powder.

When the mackerel has warmed to room temperature, brush each one on both sides with some of the garlic oil. Sprinkle generously on both sides with the salt, then pat on the spices to make a crust. Set aside.

Put the tomato quarters on a plate, cover half with the sliced garlic, and let sit for a few minutes. Drain the shallot slices, pat dry, and toss with the chardonnay vinegar and a pinch of salt.

Remove a few garlic slices from the tomatoes—this sounds fussy, but it will leave some garlic flavor without being overpowering. Divide the tomatoes among four plates, leaving room for the cooked fish. Top each serving with a few shallot slices and a sprinkling of the garnacha vinegar. Season with a pinch of salt. Lay the basil and lovage leaves over the top.

Heat a large carbon-steel or cast-iron skillet over medium-high heat. Once it's good and hot, add the olive oil, then add the fish. If you need to cook the fish in two batches, you can keep first batch warm in a 200°F (95°C) oven on a wire rack set atop a baking sheet, then give it a quick go in the pan again before serving. Cook for 2 minutes, or until golden brown on the first side, then flip and cook for 2 to 3 more minutes, until the fish has a nice golden brown crust on the second side. A cake tester inserted into the thickest part of a fish should feel warm when pressed to your lip. Just before you remove the fish, splash it with the fish sauce, both for flavor and to help release the crispy skin from the pan.

Arrange the fish next to the tomato salads and dress with the sherry vinegar. Serve immediately.

mains

These are among our favorite main course recipes. You may notice that for each main ingredient, we've landed on a versatile seasoning and cooking technique. So, for instance, you may choose to learn how we build a crust of coriander seeds and peppercorns on a piece of swordfish, or perhaps how we prepare a hanger steak, amplifying its flavor with garlic oil and fish sauce, and then incorporate those particular ideas into your own recipes.

Swordfish

The pork of the sea. Most of the time, it is brutally overcooked, but that is not the case here: As long as the quality of the product is reliable, you can keep it a little pink. The way we crust the fish works beautifully in these recipes.

Swordfish with Meyer Lemon and Heart of Palm

The first time I tried fresh hearts of palm, I actually felt cheated by having only had the ones from the can. Whatever comes in the can is fine—I should say, *barely* fine—but it has nothing to do with what they really are. Simply oven-roasted heart of palm with olive oil and salt is divine.

Serves 4

1 fresh heart of palm, about a foot long
  (see Sourcing, page 296)
2 thick swordfish steaks
  (about 1 pound/450 g total),
  cut crosswise in half and trimmed to
  remove skin, gristle, and dark parts
2 teaspoons fennel seeds
½ teaspoon black peppercorns
½ teaspoon chile flakes
1 teaspoon kosher salt, plus a pinch
2 tablespoons Garlic Oil (page 46)
About 3 tablespoons extra-virgin olive oil
2 teaspoons fish sauce
4 teaspoons sherry vinegar
3 tablespoons Egg Yolk Emulsion
  (page 50)
2 tablespoons Meyer Lemon Condiment
  (page 48)

Preheat the oven to 350°F (180°C).

Char the heart of palm over a gas flame or on a grill, turning occasionally, until you have an even char all over (be careful—if you char it too much, you risk burning the inside). Or you can skip charring and just oven-roast, if you prefer.

Cut the heart of palm in half and transfer it to a small baking dish. Sprinkle with a few teaspoons of water, cover tightly with foil, and bake for 20 minutes, or until you can easily insert a cake tester into the heart of palm. Remove from the oven and let cool.

With a spoon or the back of a paring knife, scrape the char off the heart of palm. Trim off any remaining dark bits and slice lengthwise on a mandoline into ⅛-inch-thick planks. You want 16 slices for this dish.

Remove the swordfish from the refrigerator and let it come to room temperature.

Meanwhile, prepare the spice mix: Coarsely grind the fennel seeds, peppercorns, and chile flakes separately in a spice grinder or with a mortar and pestle, then mix them together.

Rub the swordfish evenly with the salt. Brush the fish with the garlic oil, then coat with the spice mixture on one side, patting it on so it adheres well.

Preheat the broiler. To cook the swordfish, heat a large carbon-steel or cast-iron skillet over medium-high heat. Once it's good and hot, add 2 tablespoons of the olive oil to the pan, move it around the pan, then add the swordfish, spiced side down, leaving space between the pieces. Cook for 1½ minutes, then pour half the fish sauce over the swordfish to help it release from the pan (you want to retain as much of the spice crust as possible). Flip the pieces carefully and cook for another minute, or until the sides of the fish are almost fully opaque, with very little pink showing (if the swordfish is quite thin, you will want to cook it for less time). Quickly brush the fish with the remaining fish sauce and half the sherry vinegar and transfer it to a platter, flipping the pieces as you do so, then brush with the remaining sherry vinegar. Let cool slightly.

While the swordfish cools, arrange the heart of palm slices on a baking sheet in a single layer and sprinkle with a tablespoon of water, a couple of teaspoons of oil, and a pinch of salt. Run under the broiler for a minute or two; you want to heat the heart of palm through, but you don't want to cook it any further.

Once the fish is cool enough that you can touch it, slice each piece horizontally into 2 planks. There should still be a bit of pink inside. Place a pair of fish slices, seared side down, on each of four plates. Finish each plate with ½ teaspoon of the remaining garlic oil (just the oil, no garlic slices). Smear each piece of fish with a generous teaspoon of the egg yolk emulsion and top each plate with a heaping teaspoon of the Meyer lemon condiment, spreading it evenly. Shingle 4 heart of palm slices over each plate and serve.

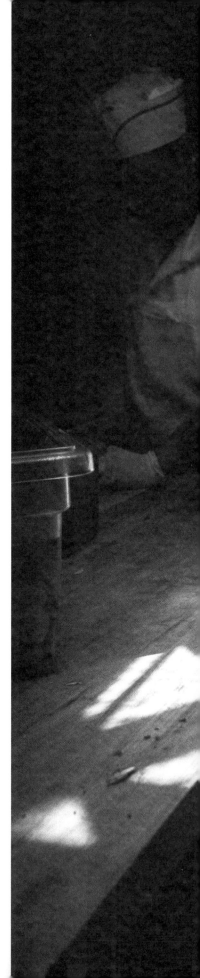

Swordfish with Meyer Lemon, Arugula, and Ajo Blanco

A perfect lunch.

Remove the swordfish from the refrigerator and let it come to room temperature.

Prepare the almonds:
Heat the olive oil in a medium skillet over medium heat for about 30 seconds, then add the almonds. Once you begin to see tiny bubbles in the pan, cook the nuts for 2 minutes longer, stirring constantly. You want them to change color only slightly; they will continue to cook a bit after you remove them from the pan, and if you cook them too much, they will become bitter. Transfer them to a paper towel–lined plate to drain. When cool, coarsely chop and toss with the salt and ground chile. They should be well spiced.

Coarsely grind the peppercorns and then the coriander seeds in a spice grinder or with a mortar and pestle. Mix together.

Rub the swordfish evenly with the kosher salt, then brush with some of the garlic oil. Coat the fish on one side only with the spice mixture, patting it on so it adheres well.

Heat a large carbon-steel or cast-iron skillet over medium-high heat. Once it's good and hot, add the olive oil, move it around the pan, then add the swordfish, spiced side down, leaving space between the pieces. Cook for 1½ minutes, then pour half the fish sauce over the fish to help it release from the pan (you want to retain as much of the spice crust as possible). Flip the pieces carefully and cook for another minute, or until the sides of the fish are almost fully opaque, with very little pink showing. (If your swordfish is quite thin, you will want to cook it for less time.) Quickly brush the fish with the remaining fish sauce and half the sherry vinegar and transfer it to a platter, flipping the pieces as you do so, then brush with the remaining sherry vinegar. Let cool slightly.

Serves 4

2 thick swordfish steaks
    (about 1 pound/450 g total),
    cut crosswise in half and trimmed to
    remove skin, gristle, and dark parts

For the Almonds
3 tablespoons extra-virgin olive oil
⅓ cup (40 g) Marcona almonds
¼ teaspoon kosher salt
¾ teaspoon chile flakes, finely ground
    (in a spice grinder or with a mortar
    and pestle)

1 tablespoon Szechuan peppercorns
1 tablespoon coriander seeds
2 teaspoons kosher salt
2 tablespoons Garlic Oil (page 46)
2 tablespoons extra-virgin olive oil
2 teaspoons fish sauce
4 teaspoons sherry vinegar
½ cup (120 ml) Ajo Blanco (page 46)
2 tablespoons Meyer Lemon Condiment
    (page 48)
4 cups (about 100 g) arugula
½ lemon
Gray salt

Once the fish is cool enough that you can touch it, slice each piece horizontally into 2 planks. There should still be a bit of pink inside.

Spoon 2 tablespoons of the ajo blanco onto each of four plates. Top each with a pair of fish slices, spiced side down. Drizzle each pair of slices with ½ teaspoon of the garlic oil (just the oil, no garlic slices). Top each portion with a heaping teaspoon of the Meyer lemon condiment, spreading it evenly over the fish. Sprinkle with the nuts, then cover the fish with the arugula. Dress the arugula on each plate with a few rasps of lemon zest, a squeeze of lemon juice, and a small pinch of gray salt. Serve.

Swordfish with Fava Bean Tabbouleh

Don't let the ingredient list scare you: The recipe is pretty easy and the tabbouleh can be done ahead of time.

Practical Note: You can make the tabbouleh up to a day ahead, but don't add the herbs until right before serving.

Make the tabbouleh:
Combine the bulgur, 1⅓ cups (320 ml) water, and a big pinch of salt in a saucepan and bring to a boil, then reduce to a simmer, cover, and cook for 12 to 15 minutes, until the bulgur is tender. Remove from the heat, drain any excess water, fluff with a fork, and let cool.

Transfer the bulgur to a bowl and add the favas, lemon, pine nuts, onion, and the remaining 2 teaspoons salt, tossing to mix. Dress with the olive oil, chardonnay vinegar, grapefruit zest, and grapefruit juice and toss again. Add the herbs, tossing gently to mix.

Remove the fish from the refrigerator and bring to room temperature.

Coarsely grind the peppercorns and then the coriander seeds in a spice grinder or with a mortar and pestle. Mix them together.

Rub the swordfish evenly with the salt. Brush the fish with the garlic oil, then coat with the spice mixture on one side, patting it on so it adheres well.

Heat a large skillet over medium-high heat. Once it's good and hot, add the olive oil, move it around the pan, then add the swordfish, spiced side down, leaving space between the pieces. Cook for 1½ minutes, then pour half the fish sauce over the fish to help it release from the pan (you want to retain as much of the spice crust as possible). Flip the pieces carefully and cook for another minute, or until the sides of the fish are almost fully opaque, with very little pink showing. (If your swordfish is quite thin, you will want to cook it for less time.) Quickly brush the fish with the remaining fish sauce and half the sherry vinegar and transfer it to a platter, flipping the pieces as you do so, then brush with the remaining sherry vinegar. Let cool slightly.

Slice each piece horizontally into 2 planks. There should still be a bit of pink inside. Spread a tablespoon of the egg yolk emulsion onto each of four serving plates. Top each with a pair of fish slices, spiced side down, and then enough tabbouleh to cover, about ¾ cup (105 g). Serve.

Serves 4

For the Tabbouleh
⅔ cup (80 g) bulgur
2 teaspoons kosher salt, plus a pinch
1 cup (175 g) blanched and peeled fava beans (from about 2 pounds/900 g in the pod), roughly chopped unless very small
¼ cup (60 g) diced lemon flesh, preferably from a Meyer lemon (it's easiest to first slice the lemon into rounds, remove peel and seeds, and then chop)
¼ cup (50 g) pine nuts
¼ cup (60 g) finely diced onion
¼ cup (60 ml) extra-virgin olive oil
1 tablespoon chardonnay vinegar
8 rasps of grapefruit zest
¼ cup (60 ml) fresh grapefruit juice
¼ cup (about 7 g) roughly chopped mint
¼ cup (about 7 g) roughly chopped lovage
¼ cup (about 7 g) roughly chopped parsley

2 thick swordfish steaks (about 1 pound/ 450 g total), cut crosswise in half and trimmed to remove skin, gristle, and dark parts
2 teaspoons Szechuan peppercorns
2 teaspoons coriander seeds
2 teaspoons kosher salt
2 tablespoons Garlic Oil (page 46)
2 tablespoons extra-virgin olive oil
2 teaspoons fish sauce
1 tablespoon plus 1 teaspoon sherry vinegar
¼ cup (60 ml) Egg Yolk Emulsion (page 50)

I first discovered tabbouleh in Brazil, where there is a sizable Lebanese community. In this version, we add grapefruit zest and juice and fava beans, and I leave out the tomatoes.

Cod

When it comes to fish, cod is the king of kings, delicate and succulent. There are other white, flaky fish that are also very delicious, such as hake and pollock, which make perfect substitutes. Skin-on fish is preferable.

Cod with Cherries and Vin Jaune Vinegar

Vin jaune vinegar will be almost impossible to source, but don't let that stop you from making this recipe. Just use vin jaune wine, which has a similarly singular oxidized quality on the nose and palate (think sherry). I find it very appealing. You may just want to add a little bit of vinegar to reinforce it.

Serves 4

For the Brine
4 cups (scant 1 l) water
½ cup (100 g) kosher salt

Four 4-ounce (115 g) pieces skin-on cod
  fillet, each about 1 inch thick

For the Marinade
6 tablespoons extra-virgin olive oil
2 tablespoons fish sauce
2 large garlic cloves, smashed
2 teaspoons coriander seeds, crushed
  under a clean heavy pan

For the Kombu Water
Half a 3½-inch square of kombu
1 cup (240 ml) water

For the Cherries
2 pounds sweet cherries, pitted
¼ cup (60 ml) vin jaune vinegar
¼ cup (60 ml) Arbequina olive oil
2 teaspoons thinly sliced Pickled Ramps
  (page 295), plus a small splash of the
  pickling liquid
Pinch of kosher salt, or to taste

About 2 tablespoons rendered pork fat,
  melted (optional)
A very small handful of dried dulse
  seaweed (preferably from Maine), torn
  into wispy pieces
A large handful of mixed aromatic but
  mild, tender leaves, such as Egyptian
  spinach, anise hyssop, shiso, sweet
  potato leaves, and/or wild spinach
Arbequina olive oil, for drizzling

Make the brine:
Combine the water and salt in a medium saucepan and bring to a boil over medium heat, stirring to dissolve the salt. Remove from the heat and let cool to room temperature.

Set the cod in a shallow baking dish just large enough to hold it and the brine comfortably. Pour the brine over the fish; it should cover the fish completely. (Alternatively, do this in a heavy-duty gallon-size zip-top bag.) Cover tightly with plastic wrap (or seal the bag) and refrigerate for 1 hour.

Make the marinade:
Combine the olive oil, fish sauce, garlic, and coriander seeds in a small bowl. Set aside.

Make the kombu water:
Put the kombu and water in a small saucepan and let soak for 15 minutes, then set the pan over medium heat, bring the water to a simmer, and simmer for 10 minutes. Remove the pan from the heat and let cool, then remove and discard the kombu. Set the kombu water aside. (This will make more than you need for this recipe, but you can use what remains for miso soup.)

Remove the fish from the baking dish and pat dry. Discard the brine and return the fish to the baking dish. Reserve about ¼ cup (60 ml) of the marinade and pour the rest of it over the fish. Marinate the cod for at least 30 minutes and up to 1 hour.

Prepare the cherries:
Juice half the cherries with a juicer. Measure out ½ cup (120 ml) of the juice and set aside.

Halve the remaining cherries and quarter any very large ones. Set aside in a small bowl.

continued

Just before cooking the fish, combine the cherry juice, vinegar, Arbequina olive oil, ramp pickling liquid, and salt in a medium bowl. Taste and adjust the seasoning if necessary, then add the cherries, tossing to combine well.

Heat a large carbon-steel or cast-iron skillet over high heat. When the pan is hot, remove the fish from the marinade, reserving the marinade, and carefully set the fish, skin side down, in the pan. Cook for about 2½ minutes, occasionally brushing with the marinade. Use a thin metal spatula to separate each piece of fillet from the skin, which will be stuck to the pan, flip the fillet over so that it rests on the stuck-on skin, and cook for 30 seconds to 1 minute, again brushing with the marinade.

Meanwhile, using a slotted spoon, divide the cherries among four shallow bowls, placing them in the center; reserve the vinaigrette left in the bowl.

Transfer the fish to the bowls, setting each over the cherries, and brush again with the marinade, as well as with some melted pork fat, if desired.

Add the dulse to the cherry vinaigrette and stir to coat, then arrange 3 or 4 pieces alongside each fillet. Sprinkle with the sliced pickled ramps. Carefully pour the vinaigrette around the fish, not onto it—it should pool around the cherries.

Very gently toss the tender leaves with a few tablespoons of the kombu water and arrange the leaves over the dulse, overlapping them slightly. Drizzle with Arbequina olive oil and serve.

Cod with Gem Lettuce, Chanterelles, and Potatoes

This is a heartier take on cod, as you have a kombu butter stock that is full and rich. The slightly wilted Gem lettuce gives a comforting and surprising sweetness, and the pickled mushrooms provide pops of freshness.

Prepare the marinated mushrooms:

About 4 hours before you plan on serving the fish, season the chanterelles with a few pinches of salt, then heat a cast-iron skillet over medium-high heat. Once it's good and hot, add the chanterelles (with no oil) and cook, tossing and moving them around with a wooden spoon, for about 2 minutes, until they are toasted on the outside and soft on the inside. Remove from the heat, add the olive oil and another pinch of salt to the pan, and toss well.

Transfer the chanterelles to a small bowl and add the garlic, anise hyssop, and enough oil to cover. Set aside.

About half an hour before cooking the fish, remove it from the refrigerator, set it on a plate, and salt both sides lightly. Let come to room temperature.

Meanwhile, put the potatoes in a medium saucepan, add water to cover generously, and salt the water until it's salty like the sea. Bring to a boil, then reduce the heat and boil gently for 20 to 25 minutes, until a cake tester inserted into a potato meets just the slightest bit of resistance (you don't want them mashed-potato soft). Drain and let cool slightly.

Peel the potatoes and cut into rough ½- to 1-inch bits with a fork. Transfer to a small bowl and toss with 1 teaspoon of the olive oil. Taste for seasoning and toss with a pinch or two of salt if needed; the potatoes should be well seasoned but not overly salty. Set aside.

Preheat the oven to 350°F (180°C).

Bring the kombu butter stock to a gentle simmer in a medium saucepan. Remove about 12 to 16 leaves from the lettuce and, working in batches, dip them into the simmering stock until they are soft and wilted. Transfer the lettuce to a shallow bowl, season with a small pinch of salt, and set aside. Keep the stock warm over low heat.

continued

Serves 4

For the Marinated Mushrooms
12 chanterelle mushrooms, cleaned and dried
Kosher salt
1 tablespoon extra-virgin olive oil, plus more as needed
1 garlic clove, smashed
3 anise hyssop leaves

Four 3½-ounce (100 g) pieces skin-on cod fillet
Kosher salt
3 medium Yukon Gold potatoes, scrubbed
About 2 tablespoons extra-virgin olive oil
1 cup (240 ml) Kombu Butter Stock (page 290)
1 head Gem lettuce, softest outer leaves removed
12 Pickled Mushrooms (page 293), with some of their onions, or store-bought pickled mushrooms

To cook the cod, add 2 teaspoons of the olive oil and then 2 pieces of cod, skin side down, to a cold ovenproof nonstick pan. (You can cook all the fish in two pans simultaneously, adding 2 teaspoons oil to the second pan, or cook them in two batches and then rewarm the first batch in the oven before serving.) Set the pan over medium heat. Once the oil starts to pop and you see bits of white fat melting out of the fish, cook for 1 more minute, then put the pan in the oven.

After 3 minutes, take the pan out, gently flip the fish over, and peel off the skin (if it doesn't come off, the fish is not cooked; give it another 30 seconds or so). To judge whether the fish is done, insert a cake tester in one piece for 10 seconds, then touch it to your lips; it should be warm, but not hot. If the cod isn't ready, pop it back into the oven for another minute. If you're cooking your fish in two batches, transfer the cooked cod to a plate and repeat with the remaining 2 pieces, then reheat the first batch in the oven before serving.

Meanwhile, drain the marinated mushrooms and rewarm them, along with the potatoes, pickled mushrooms, and lettuce, on a baking sheet in the oven for just a minute or so.

Put the fish in four shallow bowls and place the potatoes next to the fish. Top the potatoes on each bowl with 3 pickled mushrooms and 3 marinated mushrooms. Cover with 3 or 4 lettuce leaves, and pour ¼ cup (60 ml) of the kombu butter stock around the edges. Serve.

Monkfish

This is one ugly-looking fish, so ugly that they sell it facedown at markets in Spain. That said, it is great, with a distinctive, firm, and meaty texture that can handle heavy seasoning and aggressive cooking. We like to serve it with a stock made from ham scraps.

Monkfish with Brussels Sprouts and Ham Broth

In the early 2000s, it was popular to wrap monkfish in prosciutto or pancetta and roast it with loads of butter. This dish speaks to that tradition, though it's lighter. Notice how the texture of the steamed Brussels sprouts matches the flesh of the fish.

Serves 4

Four 3- to 4-ounce (85 to 115 g) pieces monkfish fillet, each 1 to 1½ inches thick
About 20 Brussels sprouts
Kosher salt
Grated zest of 1 lemon
2 tablespoons Garlic Oil (page 46)
Cracked black pepper
1 tablespoon extra-virgin olive oil
1 cup (240 ml) Ham Stock (page 292)
2 teaspoons fish sauce
4 teaspoons sherry vinegar

About half an hour before serving, take the monkfish out of the refrigerator to come to room temperature.

Trim the bottoms of the Brussels sprouts, then steam them until they are bright green and retain just a bit of crunch, 10 to 12 minutes, depending on their size. Remove from the heat and let cool slightly.

Quarter the Brussels sprouts if large and transfer to a bowl. Toss them with ½ teaspoon salt and the lemon zest. Set aside.

To cook the monkfish, heat a large carbon-steel or cast-iron skillet over medium-high heat. Brush the fish with the garlic oil, then salt it well on both sides and give it a few cracks of black pepper. Add the olive oil to the hot pan, then add the monkfish and cook, turning once, for 4 minutes on each side; flip the fish gently to preserve your crust. You may have to flip the pieces onto their sides for a minute or two if they're still looking translucent. The fish is ready when a cake tester inserted into its thickest section for 5 seconds is hot when pressed to your lip.

While the monkfish cooks, heat the ham stock in a small saucepan over medium heat.

When the fish is done, transfer it to a cutting board and splash it with the fish sauce and vinegar. Slice each piece horizontally into 2 planks.

Arrange a pair of monkfish slices, cut side up, in each of four shallow bowls. Pour ¼ cup (60 ml) of the ham stock around the edges of each pair, then distribute the Brussels sprouts over the top of the fish and serve.

Monkfish with Crab Tomalley, Potatoes, and Nettles

This particular dish has what a lot of people would call fishiness but what I prefer to describe as oceanic: confident, layered flavors, anything but bland. The potatoes help bring balance, and you will be surprised by how delicious the pickled nettles are. Finding nettles should not be an issue, because they're actually a weed.

Make the kombu broth:

Put the kombu and shiitakes in a small saucepan, add the water, and set aside to soak for about 15 minutes.

Bring the water in the saucepan just to a simmer, reduce the heat, and simmer gently for 5 minutes. Remove and discard the kombu and mushrooms.

Season the broth to taste with salt and fish sauce; it should be only lightly salty. Reduce the heat to low and add the butter a few cubes at a time, whisking lightly until the butter is just melted before adding more. The broth will become thick and glossy as you do this. Very gently fold in the crab tomalley. Set the broth aside, covered to keep warm.

Cook the potatoes:

Bring a large saucepan of water to a boil over high heat. Salt the water generously, add the bay leaf and potatoes, and boil for 12 to 15 minutes, until the potatoes are tender. Drain and set aside in a warm spot.

Make the glazing mixture:

While the potatoes cook, combine ¼ cup (60 ml) of the fish sauce, ¼ cup (60 ml) of the garlic oil, the salt, and the pepper in a small bowl; set aside. Combine the remaining ¼ cup (60 ml) each fish sauce and garlic oil and the vinegar in another small bowl. Set aside.

Heat a small skillet over medium heat. When it is hot, add the chopped pickled nettles and ramps and cook, stirring frequently, until slightly caramelized, about a minute or so. Remove from the heat and let cool slightly.

Divide the nettle-ramp mixture into thirds. Leave one-third as is, chop the second third medium-fine, and finely chop the remaining third. Transfer all the chopped nettles and ramps to a small bowl and

Serves 4

For the Kombu Broth
One 3½-inch square kombu, rinsed
2 dried shiitake mushrooms
2 cups (480 ml) water
Kosher salt
Fish sauce
7 tablespoons (100 g) unsalted butter, cubed
½ cup (about 100 g) crab tomalley (see headnote, page 136)

For the Potatoes
Kosher salt
1 bay leaf
1 pound (450 g) very small Gold Marble or other creamy potatoes

For the Glazing Mixture
½ cup (120 ml) fish sauce
½ cup (120 ml) Garlic Oil (page 46)
2 large pinches of kosher salt
Large pinch of freshly ground black pepper
¼ cup (60 ml) sherry vinegar

¼ cup (about 60 g) coarsely chopped Pickled Nettles (page 295)
1 tablespoon coarsely chopped Pickled Ramps (page 295)
1 tablespoon Arbequina olive oil
½ teaspoon grated lemon zest
Sherry vinegar
Fish sauce
1 tablespoon extra-virgin olive oil
Four 3- to 4-ounce (85 to 115 g) pieces monkfish fillet, each 1 to 1½ inches thick

add the Arbequina olive oil, lemon zest, and vinegar and fish sauce to taste. Set aside.

Heat a large carbon-steel or cast-iron skillet over high heat. Add the extra-virgin olive oil, then add the monkfish and cook, brushing regularly with the glazing mixture and turning the fish once, for about 4 minutes on each side. You may have to flip the pieces onto their sides for a minute or two if they're still looking translucent. The fish is ready when a cake tester inserted into its thickest section for 5 seconds is hot when pressed to your lip.

Transfer the fish to a cutting board and slice each piece horizontally into 2 planks.

To serve, arrange a pair of monkfish slices, cut side up, in each of four shallow bowls. Dress each serving of fish with a spoonful of the glazing mixture. Divide the potatoes among the bowls, arranging them next to the fish. Pour the kombu broth over the potatoes and fish, then garnish with the chopped pickled nettles and ramps.

Monkfish with Cabbage and Chestnuts

I can't think of anything we serve that's more suited for a cold night.

Serves 4

Four 3- to 4-ounce (85 to 115 g) pieces
    monkfish fillet, each 1 to 1½ inches
    thick
1 cone cabbage
Kosher salt
About 5 teaspoons extra-virgin olive oil
5 tablespoons (75 ml) sherry vinegar
2 tablespoons Garlic Oil (page 46)
Cracked black pepper
1 cup (240 ml) Ham Stock (page 292)
2 teaspoons fish sauce
¼ cup (about 60 g) Chestnut Condiment
    (page 48)

About half an hour before serving, take the monkfish out of the refrigerator to come to room temperature.

Preheat the broiler to high. Cut the cabbage into 8 wedges and season them generously with salt—a few teaspoons total. Lay them on a baking sheet and drizzle with a teaspoon or two of water and the same amount of olive oil. Place under the broiler and cook, flipping the cabbage once, until its cut faces are charred and the leaves are cooked through but not wilted. Remove from the oven and dress with a couple of teaspoons of vinegar. (You can keep the cabbage warm in a low oven while the fish cooks.)

To cook the fish, heat a large carbon-steel or cast-iron skillet over medium-high heat. Brush the fish with the garlic oil, then salt it well on both sides and give it a few cracks of black pepper. Add a tablespoon of olive oil to the pan, then add the monkfish and cook, turning once, for 4 minutes on each side; flip the fish gently to preserve the crust. You may have to flip the pieces onto their sides for a minute or two if they're still looking translucent. The fish is ready when a cake tester inserted into its thickest section for 5 seconds is hot when pressed to your lip.

While the fish cooks, rewarm the ham stock in a small saucepan over medium-low heat.

When the fish is done, transfer it to a cutting board and splash it with the fish sauce and the remaining vinegar. Slice each piece horizontally into 2 planks.

Arrange a pair of monkfish slices, cut side up, in each of four shallow bowls. Place a tablespoon of the chestnut condiment between the slices in each bowl, then top each with 2 cabbage wedges. Pour ¼ cup (60 ml) of the ham stock around the edges of each serving and serve.

Monkfish with Asparagus and "Béarnaise"

As simple as this may seem, the level of care you put into the execution is essential. You can shave some bottarga or mojama on top, or even some black truffles if you're feeling fancy.

About half an hour before serving, take the monkfish out of the refrigerator to come to room temperature.

Meanwhile, preheat the broiler.

Snap off the woody ends of the asparagus stalks and wash the stalks well, then slice each one in half lengthwise.

Put the asparagus on a baking sheet and toss with a pinch of salt, a few drops of water, and a teaspoon of the olive oil. Spread out the asparagus and broil for 2 minutes, or until they have a bit of color on them and are just beginning to get tender. Remove from the oven and set aside.

To cook the fish, heat a large carbon-steel or cast-iron skillet over medium-high heat. Brush the fish with the garlic oil, then salt it well on both sides and give it a few cracks of black pepper. Add the remaining 3 teaspoons olive oil to the pan, then add the monkfish and cook, turning once, for 4 minutes on each side; flip the fish gently to preserve the crust. You may have to flip the pieces onto their sides for a minute or two if they're still looking translucent. The fish is ready when a cake tester inserted into its thickest section for 5 seconds is hot when pressed to your lip.

While the fish cooks, gently rewarm the asparagus in a large skillet over medium-low heat.

When the fish is done, transfer it to a cutting board and splash it with fish sauce and the vinegar. Slice each piece horizontally into 2 planks.

To serve, arrange a pair of monkfish slices, cut side up, in each of four shallow bowls. Spoon the béarnaise over the fish, then arrange 6 pieces of asparagus on top.

Serves 4

Four 3- to 4-ounce (85 to 115 g) pieces monkfish fillet, each 1 to 1½ inches thick
12 asparagus stalks
Kosher salt
4 teaspoons extra-virgin olive oil
2 tablespoons Garlic Oil (page 46)
Cracked black pepper
Fish sauce
4 teaspoons sherry vinegar
About 5 tablespoons (75 ml) Béarnaise (page 50), warm

Quail

My favorite bird. With only a mild gaminess, it lets me meet the desire for chicken while keeping things interesting. Each person is served a whole bird, which makes using your hands pretty much inevitable.

In any case, the trick is drying the bird for at least a day or more in the refrigerator, which will allow the skin to cook better. Indeed, you could try this with other birds. In these recipes, we butterfly and broil for ease, but you could pan-roast or char-grill.

While these recipes call for four quail, it never hurts to have an extra one or two.

Quail with Peas and Lardo

Best made this way when you have access to the freshest sweet peas. I would recommend that as you clean the peas, you choose the most tender ones for gentle cooking. For the starchier ones, cook separately and longer; when ready to serve the dish, mash those up with some lardo and spread onto toast.

Serves 4

4 quail (about 4 ounces/115 g each), patted dry
Extra-virgin olive oil
Kosher salt
Cracked black pepper
2 garlic cloves
Leaves from a few sprigs of rosemary
¼ cup (60 ml) fish sauce
About ½ cup (100 g) cubed (¼-inch) lardo
1 cup (175 g) shelled fresh peas

Practical Note: You will need to dry the quail at least one day ahead.

With scissors or a sharp knife, cut down one side of each quail's spine to butterfly it, then open it out and press to flatten the bird. Check the insides to make sure everything has been cleared out—you'll likely want to pull out some of the blood vessels you see. Place the quail, skin side up, on a baking sheet or platter and let them dry out, uncovered, in the fridge overnight to ensure crispy skin.

The next day, rub each quail all over with a teaspoon or two of olive oil, then season on both sides with salt and cracked black pepper. Let sit, skin side up, on a wire rack set over a baking sheet for 20 minutes or so to come to room temperature.

Meanwhile, mince the garlic and finely chop the rosemary. Combine with the fish sauce in a small bowl.

Preheat the broiler to high, with the rack as close to the flame as you can get it.

Lacquer each bird with some of the fish sauce mixture, then place the quail under the broiler for about 5 minutes, lacquering once or twice more as they cook. For even cooking, you may have to move the pan or rotate it once or twice, depending on your broiler. Once the skin is golden and crispy, flip the quail and cook on the other side for a minute or so, until cooked through. When done, the juices should run clear and a cake tester inserted into the flesh near the neck/shoulder should come out warm, but not hot. Chubbier birds may need an extra minute or so under the broiler.

While the quail cook, warm the lardo in a small saucepan over medium-low heat for 30 seconds to 1 minute, until it begins to soften and turn translucent. Add the peas and a splash of water to help them cook and cook until they are bright green and no longer raw tasting, about 2 minutes. Season with a pinch of salt. To serve, arrange a quail on each of four plates and plate a pile of the pea mixture next to each one.

Quail with Mashed Squash and Brown Butter on Toast

This is a friendly dish. You'll end up with more squash than you need, so I encourage you to double up on the toast.

Serves 4

4 quail (about 4 ounces/115 g each),
    patted dry

For the Mashed Squash
1 small butternut squash, halved
    lengthwise and seeds and membranes
    scooped out
1 tablespoon extra-virgin olive oil
Kosher salt
2 tablespoons unsalted butter

Extra-virgin olive oil
Kosher salt
Cracked black pepper
4 thin slices miche, cut into 3¾ by
    1½-inch squares
3 garlic cloves
Leaves from a few sprigs of rosemary
¼ cup (60 ml) fish sauce
1 cup (240 ml) Chicken Jus (page 289)

Practical Note: You will need to dry the quail at least one day before preparing the recipe.

With scissors or a sharp knife, cut down one side of each quail's spine to butterfly it, then open it out and press to flatten the bird. Check the insides to make sure everything has been cleared out—you'll likely want to pull out some of the blood vessels you see. Place the quail, skin side up, on a baking sheet or platter and let them dry out, uncovered, in the fridge overnight to ensure crispy skin.

The next day, preheat the oven to 350°F (180°C).

Make the squash:
Rub the butternut squash flesh with the olive oil and season generously with salt. Put it, cut side down, on a parchment-lined baking sheet and bake for 1 hour, or until the squash is cooked through and soft. Remove from the oven and let cool slightly.

Meanwhile, melt the butter in a small saucepan over medium heat and cook until it turns a nutty golden brown and smells toasty and fragrant. Take it off the heat and pour it into a small cup. As it cools, the dark bits will settle to the bottom. Transfer the browned butter to another cup, leaving the browned milk solids behind.

Scoop the flesh of the squash into a bowl. Stir in the browned butter, mixing well. Taste for seasoning—if the squash is bland, add a bit of salt. Transfer 1 cup (or more if you'd like) of the mash to a small saucepan and set aside. Cover and refrigerate the remaining for another time (see the headnote).

Rub each quail all over with a teaspoon or two of olive oil, then season on both sides with salt and cracked black pepper. Let sit, skin side up, on a wire rack set over a baking sheet for 20 minutes or so to come to room temperature.

Meanwhile, heat a large carbon-steel or cast-iron skillet over medium-high heat, then add a bit of olive oil—no more than a teaspoon or two. Add the bread slices and let them char, pressing down on them gently with a metal spatula or the clean bottom of a pan. Flip once you have a good bit of black on each slice and char on the second side. When both sides are charred, remove the bread and quickly rub each slice with a garlic clove; ideally the garlic should sizzle a bit when you do so.

Mince the remaining 2 garlic cloves and finely chop the rosemary. Combine with the fish sauce in a small bowl.

Preheat the broiler to high, with the rack as close to the flame as you can get it.

Lacquer each bird with some of the fish sauce mixture, then place the quail under the broiler for about 5 minutes, lacquering once or twice more as they cook. For even cooking, you may have to move the pan or rotate it once or twice, depending on your broiler. Once the skin is golden and crispy, flip the quail and cook on the other side for a minute or so, until cooked through. When done, the juices should run clear and a cake tester inserted into the flesh near the neck/shoulder should come out warm, but not hot. Chubbier birds may need an extra minute or so under the broiler.

While the quail cooks, reheat the squash over medium-low heat, stirring occasionally. Heat the chicken jus in a small saucepan over medium-low heat.

To serve, spread ¼ cup (about 50 g) of the squash over each piece of toast and place one in each of four shallow bowls. Top with the quail. Pour ¼ cup (60 ml) of the chicken jus around each serving.

Quail with Green Beans, Dijon, and Almonds

I love the combination of green beans and nuts, and I love mustard, and I love crispy birds—that was more or less the thought process that went into this dish.

Practical Note: You will need to dry the quail at least one day before preparing the recipe.

With scissors or a sharp knife, cut down one side of each quail's spine to butterfly it, then open it out and press on it to flatten the bird. Check the insides to make sure everything has been cleared out—you'll likely want to pull out some of the blood vessels you see. Place the quail, skin side up, on a baking sheet or large platter and let them dry out, uncovered, in the fridge overnight. (This will help ensure crispy skin.)

The next day, rub each quail all over with a teaspoon or two of olive oil, then season on both sides with kosher salt and cracked black pepper. Let sit, skin side up, on a wire rack set over a baking sheet for 20 minutes or so to come to room temperature.

Meanwhile, bring a large pot of salted water (it should be saltier than the sea, and the taste should almost shock you when you taste it) to a boil. Prepare an ice bath.

Mince the garlic and finely chop the rosemary. Combine with the fish sauce in a small bowl.

Mix together the mustards in a small bowl, then stream in a generous tablespoon of olive oil.

Once the water comes to a rolling boil, add the green beans and blanch for 2 minutes; they should be a vibrant green and still retain a bit of crunch. Drain them and transfer them to the ice bath. Once they have cooled, drain them and pat dry. Season with a few pinches of kosher salt, the lemon zest, lemon juice, and the vinegar. Toss with the mustard-oil mixture. Set aside.

Pour 2 tablespoons olive oil into a medium skillet set over medium-low heat. Add the almonds, and once they start gently bubbling, cook, stirring regularly, for 2 minutes longer, or until they are a very light golden color. (They will continue to cook once you remove

Serves 4

4 quail (about 4 ounces/115 g each), patted dry
Extra-virgin olive oil
Kosher salt
Cracked black pepper
2 garlic cloves
Leaves from a few sprigs of rosemary
¼ cup (60 ml) fish sauce
2 teaspoons grainy mustard
2 teaspoons Dijon mustard
12 ounces (340 g) green beans, trimmed
Grated zest of 1 lemon
2 teaspoons fresh lemon juice
2 teaspoons chardonnay vinegar
½ cup (50 g) Marcona almonds
¼ teaspoon flaky salt
1 cup (240 ml) Chicken Jus (page 289)

them from the pan.) Transfer them to a paper towel–lined plate to drain, then sprinkle with the flaky salt and roughly chop.

Preheat the broiler to high, with the rack as close to the flame as you can get it.

Lacquer each bird with some of the fish sauce mixture, then place the quail under the broiler for about 5 minutes, lacquering once or twice more as they cook. For even cooking, you may have to move the pan or rotate it once or twice, depending on your broiler. Once the skin is golden and crispy, flip the quail and cook on the other side for a minute or so, until cooked through. When done, the juices should run clear and a cake tester inserted into the flesh near the neck/shoulder should come out warm, but not hot. Chubbier birds may need an extra minute or so under the broiler.

While the quail cooks, heat the chicken jus in a small saucepan over medium-low heat.

To serve, toss the green beans with the almonds. Arrange a quail in each of four shallow bowls and place a pile of beans next to each bird. Pour ¼ cup (60 ml) of the chicken jus around each serving.

Just a pretty picture of charred peppers for Romesco (page 41)

Pork

Pork butt is an inexpensive cut full of character that is usually reserved for braises and other slow cooking. We like to prepare it quickly in a hot skillet (or on a grill). In order to make this possible, we tenderize it with a tool that looks like a medieval instrument of torture. There are a few other important steps, like brining overnight and marinating for 6 to 12 hours—it requires some patience but will make the result juicy and perfect.

A reminder: Feel free to plate all these dishes however you like. Don't feel as if you have to play our game of peekaboo.

Pork with Charred Cucumbers and Leeks

As we have seen already (see page 117), charring and marinating cucumbers gives them an interesting, almost meaty, yet still fresh quality. Doing the same to leeks makes them both savory and sweet. As in all of these pork recipes, the sauce, which is actually chicken jus, brings it all together.

Serves 4

For the Pork
4½ cups (1.1 l) water
⅓ cup (70 g) kosher salt, plus a pinch
One 20-ounce (570 g) piece trimmed
    pork butt (about 3½ by 3½ by
    1½ inches high), cut into 4 portions
2 garlic cloves
Zest of 1 lemon, removed in strips with
    a vegetable peeler
1 teaspoon chile flakes
2 sprigs thyme
½ cup (120 ml) extra-virgin olive oil

For the Vegetables
3 Persian cucumbers
2 large leeks, trimmed
2 teaspoons extra-virgin olive oil
1 tablespoon sherry vinegar
2 teaspoons Green Garlic Juice
    (page 46)
1 tablespoon fish sauce
Pinch of kosher salt

2 tablespoons extra-virgin olive oil
1 cup (240 ml) Chicken Jus (page 289)
8 anchovy fillets, mashed to an almost-
    smooth paste

Practical Note: You will need to brine the pork overnight before preparing the recipe, and then marinate it for at least 6 hours more.

Prepare the pork:
Combine the water and salt in a plastic or other nonreactive container, stirring to dissolve the salt. Add the pork, making sure it's fully submerged (add more water if necessary), and brine in the refrigerator for 12 hours.

The next day, using a mortar and pestle, pound the garlic until it's broken down into wisps and small bits, but not to a paste. Add the lemon zest, chile flakes, and thyme and gently pound everything together to release the oils from the zest. Add the olive oil and mix to combine the marinade.

Remove the pork from the brine and use a meat tenderizer—the kind with blades, not a mallet—to tenderize each piece: Press it down 3 or 4 times into the harder, fattier, more sinewy parts of the meat. Be gently brutal. You don't want to damage the meat. Transfer the pork to another container, add the marinade, turning to coat, and marinate in the refrigerator for 6 to 12 hours.

An hour or so before you are ready to cook, remove the pork from the marinade, pat dry, and set aside on a plate to come to room temperature.

Prepare the vegetables:
Char the cucumbers and leeks over a gas flame at very high heat or on a grill, turning them frequently. You want to almost entirely blacken the outsides, but you don't want the inner flesh to burn. The leeks should be a little more blackened than the cucumbers and should feel a little soft when you squeeze them. Let cool. Once the vegetables are cool, use a paring knife to scrape off the blackened bits of the cucumbers; this will take some patience. Slice them crosswise in half and then lengthwise into quarters, so you have little spears. Peel the most blackened layer off the leeks, and slice those

into spears as well. Ideally the cucumber and leek spears should be about the same length.

Combine the olive oil, the vinegar, green garlic juice, fish sauce, and salt in a small bowl. Put the leeks and cucumbers in two separate bowls and pour the marinade over them, dividing it evenly and turning to coat. Let marinate for 20 to 25 minutes at room temperature. The vegetables should taste well seasoned.

When you are ready to cook the pork, turn on your broiler and pop the leeks and cucumbers in there for a few minutes to warm them.

Heat a large carbon-steel or cast-iron skillet over medium-high heat for about 5 minutes. Add the oil to the pan and let it heat up, then add the pork. (You'll have to do this in two batches if your pan isn't big enough; or use two pans.) Press each piece down to get a good, even sear and let cook for 3 minutes. Flip and cook for another 3 minutes. Finish by flipping them onto their sides for 10 to 20 seconds each. Be sure to brown the edges. The pork should be medium-rare, nice and pink on the inside—a cake tester inserted into the center for 10 seconds should come out warm, but not hot (around 145°F/65°C if you have a thermometer). If you like, you can insert a knife into the side of the meat to make sure it's not underdone. Transfer the pork to a cutting board, cover loosely with foil, and let rest for 10 minutes.

Meanwhile, heat the chicken jus in a small saucepan over medium heat.

Slice each piece of pork horizontally in half into 2 planks. Smear about 1 teaspoon of the anchovy paste on the cooked side of each plank.

To serve, place 2 slices of pork, cut side up, in each of four shallow bowls, then top with the leeks and cucumbers. We like to alternate the leeks with the cucumbers, with the longest pieces in the middle and the shortest on the sides. Pour ¼ cup (60 ml) of the jus around each serving.

Pork with Potato Chips and "Borani"

In other words, pork, salty potatoes, and an intensely herbal dip. If you don't want chips, boiled or roasted potatoes are a fine substitution.

Serves 4

For the Pork
4½ cups (1.1 l) water
⅓ cup (70 g) kosher salt
One 20-ounce (570 g) piece trimmed pork butt (about 3½ by 3½ by 1½ inches high), cut into 4 portions
2 garlic cloves
Zest of 1 lemon, removed in strips with a vegetable peeler
1 teaspoon chile flakes
2 sprigs thyme
½ cup (120 ml) extra-virgin olive oil

2 tablespoons extra-virgin olive oil
1 cup (240 ml) Chicken Jus (page 289)
8 anchovy fillets mashed to an almost-smooth paste
About 1 cup (240 ml) Borani (recipe follows)
Potato Chips (page 52)

Practical Note: You will need to brine the pork overnight before preparing the recipe, and then marinate it for at least 6 hours more.

Prepare the pork:
Combine the water and salt in a plastic or other nonreactive container, stirring to dissolve the salt. Add the pork, making sure it's fully submerged (add more water if necessary), and brine in the refrigerator for 12 hours.

The next day, using a mortar and pestle, pound the garlic until it's broken down into wisps and small bits, but not to a paste. Add the lemon zest, chile flakes, and thyme and gently pound everything together to release the oils from the zest. Add the olive oil and mix to combine the marinade.

Remove the pork from the brine and use a meat tenderizer—the kind with blades, not a mallet—to tenderize each piece: Press it down 3 or 4 times into the harder, fattier, more sinewy parts of the meat. Be gently brutal. You don't want to damage the meat. Transfer the pork to another container, add the marinade, turning to coat, and marinate in the refrigerator for 6 to 12 hours.

An hour or so before you're ready to cook, remove the pork from the marinade, pat dry, and set aside on a plate to come to room temperature.

Heat a large carbon-steel or cast-iron skillet over medium-high heat for about 5 minutes. Once it's good and hot, add the olive oil to the pan and let it heat up, then add the pork. (You'll have to do this in two batches if your pan isn't big enough; or use two pans.) Press each piece down to get a good, even sear, then let cook for 3 minutes. Flip and cook for 3 minutes more. Finish by flipping the pieces of pork onto their sides for 10 to 20 seconds for each side. Be sure to brown the edges. The pork should be medium-rare, nice and pink on the inside—a cake tester inserted into the center for 10 seconds should come out warm, but not hot (around 145°F/65°C if you have a thermometer). If you like, you can insert a knife into the side of the meat to make sure it's not underdone. Transfer the pork to a cutting board, cover loosely with foil, and let rest for 10 minutes.

Meanwhile, heat the chicken jus in a small saucepan over medium heat.

Slice each piece of pork horizontally in half into 2 planks. Smear about 1 teaspoon of the anchovy paste on the cooked side of each plank.

To serve, place about ¼ cup (60 ml) of the borani in each of four shallow bowls, then top with 2 pork slices, cut side up. Cover with potato chips – break larger ones in half – then pour ¼ cup (60 ml) of the chicken jus around each serving.

Borani

Makes about 2 cups (480 ml)

1 large bunch cilantro, trimmed
2 cups (480 ml) full-fat Greek yogurt
1½ cups (about 350 g) chopped Pickled Ramps (page 295)
2 tablespoons roughly chopped lovage stems and leaves
Grated zest of ½ lemon
1 teaspoon sugar
1 garlic clove, grated
Kosher salt

Finely chop enough of the cilantro leaves and small stems to make 1 cup; set aside. Using a juicer, juice the remaining cilantro. You want 1 teaspoon juice for the borani.

Put the yogurt in a bowl and stir in the cilantro juice, then stir in the chopped cilantro and all the remaining ingredients. Taste and adjust the seasoning if necessary. Cover and refrigerate until ready to serve.

Pork with Cabbage, Wheat Berries, and Juniper Berries

Think of pork and sauerkraut, if you need a reference.

Practical Notes: You will need to brine the pork overnight before preparing the recipe, and then marinate it for at least 6 hours more.

We source our wheat berries from Anson Mills in North Carolina.

Prepare the pork:
Combine the water and salt in a plastic or other nonreactive container, stirring to dissolve the salt. Add the pork, making sure it's fully submerged (add more water if necessary), and brine in the refrigerator for 12 hours.

The next day, using a mortar and pestle, pound the garlic cloves until broken down into wisps and small bits, but not to a paste. Add the lemon zest, chile flakes, and thyme and gently pound everything together to release the oils from the zest. Add the olive oil and mix to combine the marinade.

Remove the pork from the brine and use a meat tenderizer—the kind with blades, not a mallet—to tenderize each piece: Press it down 3 or 4 times into the harder, fattier, more sinewy parts of the meat. Be gently brutal. You don't want to damage the meat. Transfer the pork to another container, add the marinade, turning to coat, and marinate in the refrigerator for 6 to 12 hours.

An hour or so before you're ready to cook, remove the pork from the marinade, pat dry, and set aside on a plate to come to room temperature.

Meanwhile, put the wheat berries in a small pot and add enough water to cover them by a few inches. Salt the water lightly and bring to a boil, then reduce the heat to a simmer and cook for 25 to 30 minutes, until the berries are softened but still toothsome. Let them cool in their cooking water, then drain.

Using a mortar and pestle, smash the juniper berries with the garlic into a rough paste. Set aside.

When ready to cook the pork, heat the broiler to high. Cut the cabbage into 8 wedges and season them generously with salt.

continued

Serves 4

For the Pork
4½ cups (1.1 l) water
⅓ cup (70 g) kosher salt
One 20-ounce (570 g) piece trimmed pork butt (about 3½ by 3½ by 1½ inches high), cut into 4 portions
2 garlic cloves
Zest of 1 lemon, removed in strips with a vegetable peeler
1 teaspoon chile flakes
2 sprigs thyme
½ cup (120 ml) extra-virgin olive oil

½ cup (75 g) wheat berries or farro or another grain
Kosher salt
2 teaspoons pickled juniper berries, or 1 tablespoon capers
½ garlic clove
1 cone cabbage
Extra-virgin olive oil
Generous 1 tablespoon sherry vinegar
¼ cup (55 g) finely diced onion
1 cup (240 ml) Chicken Jus (page 289)

Lay the wedges on a baking sheet and drizzle with a teaspoon or two of water and the same amount of olive oil. Place under the broiler and cook, flipping the cabbage once, until its cut faces are charred and the leaves are cooked but not soft. Remove from the oven and toss with the vinegar. (You can keep the cabbage warm in a low oven while the pork cooks.)

Meanwhile, combine the wheat berries, a drizzle of olive oil, a splash of water, and the onion in a saucepan and cook over medium-low heat, stirring occasionally, until the wheat berries are warm and the onion has softened.

Heat a large carbon-steel or cast-iron skillet over medium-high heat for about 5 minutes. Add 2 tablespoons olive oil to the pan and let it heat up, then add the pork. (You'll have to do this in two batches if your pan isn't big enough; or use two pans.) Press each piece down to get a good, even sear, then let cook for 3 minutes. Flip and cook for 3 minutes more. Finish by flipping the pieces of pork onto their sides for 10 to 20 seconds each. Be sure to brown the edges. The pork should be medium-rare, nice and pink on the inside—a cake tester inserted into the center for 10 seconds should come out warm, but not hot (around 145°F/65°C if you have a thermometer). If you like, you can insert a knife into the side of the meat to make sure it's not underdone. Transfer the pork to a cutting board, cover loosely with foil, and let rest for 10 minutes.

Meanwhile, heat the chicken jus in a small saucepan over medium heat.

Slice each piece of pork horizontally in half into 2 planks. Smear a bit of the juniper-garlic paste on the cooked side of each plank.

To serve, place 2 pork slices, seared side down, in each of four shallow bowls, then top with the wheat berries. Arrange 2 cabbage wedges on each plate. Pour ¼ cup (60 ml) of the chicken jus around each serving.

Pork with Greens and Truffles

This is actually all about the greens and the sauce. And trust me, you'll want a lot of this sauce. The black truffles are merely there to add a delicate earthy and woodsy note. Feel free to replace them with shaved dried shiitake mushrooms, which you may have on hand from preparing one of our stocks.

Serves 4

For the Pork
4½ cups (1.1 l) water
⅓ cup (70 g) kosher salt
One 20-ounce (570 g) piece trimmed pork butt (about 3½ by 3½ by 1½ inches high), cut into 4 portions
2 large garlic cloves
Zest of 1 lemon, removed in strips with a vegetable peeler
1 heaping teaspoon chile flakes
2 sprigs thyme
½ cup (120 ml) extra-virgin olive oil

1 large garlic clove, crushed
1 teaspoon dried yuzu zest (or substitute 1 tablespoon mixed grated lemon and lime zests)
1 tablespoon vadouvan curry powder
Splash of sherry vinegar
1½ tablespoons fish sauce
4 tablespoons extra-virgin olive oil
2 cups (480 ml) Ham Stock (page 292)
½ cup (120 ml) white wine, such as Müller-Thurgau, vinho verde, or another light, fresh, dry wine
½ pound (2 sticks; 225 g) unsalted butter
1 tablespoon very finely diced black winter truffle, plus 1 heaping teaspoon truffle trimmings
Grapeseed oil
A large handful of mixed mild, tender leaves, such as baby kale, sorrel, sweet potato leaves, and/or torn Swiss chard

Practical Note: You will need to brine the pork overnight before preparing the recipe, and then marinate it for at least 6 hours more.

Prepare the pork:
Combine the water and salt in a plastic or other nonreactive container, stirring to dissolve the salt. Add the pork, making sure it is fully submerged (add more water if necessary), and brine in the refrigerator for 12 hours.

The next day, using a mortar and pestle, pound the garlic cloves until broken down into wisps and small bits, but not to a paste. Add the lemon zest, chile flakes, and thyme and gently pound everything together to release the oils from the zest. Add the olive oil and mix to combine the marinade.

Remove the pork from the brine and use a meat tenderizer—the kind with blades, not a mallet—to tenderize each piece: Press it down 3 or 4 times into the harder, fattier, more sinewy parts of the meat. Be gently brutal. You don't want to damage the meat. Transfer the pork to another container, add the marinade, turning to coat, and marinate in the refrigerator for 6 to 12 hours.

An hour before cooking, remove the pork from the marinade and pat dry. Set on a plate and allow to come to room temperature.

Meanwhile, combine the garlic, yuzu zest, vadouvan, sherry vinegar, fish sauce, and 2 tablespoons of the olive oil in a small bowl. Set aside.

Just before cooking the pork, pour the ham stock into a small saucepan and bring just to a simmer. Reduce the heat to medium-low and add the wine, then whisk in the butter a few pieces at a time, waiting until each addition has almost melted before adding more, until the sauce is emulsified. Reduce the heat to the lowest possible setting and cover to keep warm.

continued

Heat a large carbon-steel or cast-iron skillet over medium-high heat for about 5 minutes. Add the remaining 2 tablespoons olive oil to the pan and let it heat up, then add the pork. (You'll have to do this in two batches if your pan isn't big enough; or use two pans.) Press each piece down to get a good, even sear, then let cook for 3 minutes. Flip and cook for 3 minutes more, brushing periodically with the vadouvan-yuzu mixture. Finish by flipping the pieces of pork onto their sides for 10 to 20 seconds a side. Be sure to brown the edges. The pork should be medium-rare, nice and pink on the inside—a cake tester inserted into the center for 10 seconds should come out warm, but not hot (around 145°/65°C if you have a thermometer). If you like, you can insert a knife into the side of the meat to make sure it's not underdone. Transfer the pork to a cutting board, cover loosely with foil, and let rest for 10 minutes.

While the pork rests, using a mortar and pestle, crush the black truffle trimmings with a few drops of grapeseed oil to a thick but spreadable paste.

Transfer the pork to a cutting board and slice each piece horizontally in half into 2 planks.

To serve, place 2 slices of pork, cut side up, in each of four shallow bowls. Spread the truffle paste over the cut sides of the pork and sprinkle the diced truffles over the meat. Top with the leaves, arranging them so they cover each piece of pork entirely. Pour ½ cup (120 ml) of the sauce around each serving.

You may use diced truffles, as the recipe indicates, or whole slices, or no truffles at all.

Steak

Everybody everywhere has their ideas, rules, and doctrines about cooking steak—whether to season before or after, whether to season with just salt or with salt and pepper, whether to move the meat as it cooks or to let it be.

Our way is simple and unorthodox. We layer flavors as we cook the meat by lacquering it, often with fish sauce and garlic oil.

Steak with Brussels Sprouts and Taleggio

The typical move would be to cook the Brussels sprouts in butter until they were totally soft, but here they are only gently steamed to preserve their character and bite—you need something clean to contrast with the sultry Taleggio and the boldly seasoned steak.

Serves 4

2 pounds (900 g) hanger steak, tough sinew removed, cut into 4 portions (ask your butcher to do this)
Kosher salt
¼ cup (60 ml) fish sauce
2 garlic cloves, minced
2 tablespoons minced rosemary
About 20 Brussels sprouts
Grated zest of 1 lemon
2 tablespoons extra-virgin olive oil
¾ cup (180 ml) Taleggio Sauce (page 37)
About 1½ tablespoons Marjoram-Anchovy Salsa Verde (page 42)
Coarse grinds of black pepper

Let your steak come to room temperature, about 30 minutes.

Coat all the pieces of steak with a generous layer of salt on all sides, really patting it into the flesh. Let sit for another 30 minutes. It may look as if it's beginning to dry out, and that's a good thing; it means you'll get a better sear.

Meanwhile, mix together the fish sauce, garlic, and rosemary in a small bowl.

Trim the bottoms of the Brussels sprouts. Steam them until they are bright green and retain just a bit of crunch, 10 to 12 minutes, depending on their size. Let cool a bit, then quarter if large and toss them in a bowl with ½ teaspoon salt and the lemon zest. Set aside.

When you're ready to cook the steak, heat a large carbon-steel or cast-iron skillet over medium-high heat for about 5 minutes. Add the olive oil to the pan, then add the steaks, gently pressing them down to get even contact and a good sear, and let cook for 2 minutes. (You'll have to do this in two batches if your pan isn't big enough; or use two pans.) Lacquer each piece with two or three brushes of the fish sauce mixture, then flip. Cook on the second side for 2 minutes, then lacquer with more fish sauce and flip again. After a minute, lacquer with more fish sauce and flip. Cook for another minute, brush again, and flip. If you have an instant-read thermometer, use it to test your steaks' internal temperature; it should be about 125°F (52°C). If you don't have a thermometer, a cake tester inserted into the interior of the steak for 10 seconds should come out warm. When the steaks are done, let them rest for 5 minutes, ideally propped up on something—like chopsticks laid over a plate—to keep the bottoms from steaming. Set the pan aside.

While the steaks rest, gently warm the Taleggio sauce.

Just before serving, heat the same skillet over medium heat and lightly sear your steaks again to warm them up, about 30 seconds on each side. Remove from the pan and slice each steak horizontally

in half into 2 planks. Coat each seared side with a generous
½ teaspoon of the salsa verde.

To serve, spoon 3 tablespoons of the Taleggio sauce onto each of
four plates, then place 2 steak slices, pink side up, on the sauce. Top
with the Brussels sprouts and a grind of black pepper.

Steak with Eggplants, Leeks, and Taleggio

The critic Alan Richman—a legendary, "opinionated" critic—once called this the best steak in America. I now remember that at the beginning, we didn't tell guests about the flavor-improving anchovies in the recipe and actually used to hide the fillets in nooks within the eggplant slices. They never noticed. As they say in my part of the world on matters more serious, *Ojos que no ven, corazón que no siente* ("Your heart doesn't hurt if you never find out").

Serves 4

2 pounds (900 g) hanger steak, tough sinew removed, cut into 4 portions (ask your butcher to do this)
Kosher salt
¼ cup (60 ml) plus 3 tablespoons fish sauce
2 garlic cloves, minced
2 tablespoons minced rosemary
2 medium leeks, trimmed
4 small to medium Japanese or Fairy Tale eggplants
¼ cup (60 ml) plus 2 tablespoons sherry vinegar
1 tablespoon plus 1 teaspoon Green Garlic Juice (page 46)
2 tablespoons extra-virgin olive oil, plus a little for drizzling
Leaves from 2 sprigs marjoram or oregano
¼ cup (60 ml) Taleggio Sauce (page 37)
About 1½ tablespoons Marjoram-Anchovy Salsa Verde (page 42)
8 anchovy fillets

Practical Note: Eggplants with a low water content will retain their structure and won't get too mushy.

Let your steaks come to room temperature, about 30 minutes.

Coat all the pieces of steak with a generous layer of salt on all sides, really patting it into the flesh. Let sit for another 30 minutes. It may look as if it's beginning to dry out, and that's a good thing; it means you'll get a better sear.

Meanwhile, mix together ¼ cup (60 ml) of the fish sauce, the garlic, and rosemary in a small bowl; set aside.

Over a gas flame or on a grill, char the leeks, turning occasionally, until the outer layer is black all around but they're not totally soft all the way through. Char the eggplants, turning, until they're well blackened and softened but still have some structure. Let the vegetables cool.

Peel off the black and brown bits. Slice the leeks into ½-inch-thick coins. Cut the eggplants lengthwise in half, then cut each piece crosswise in half.

Put the leeks in a bowl and toss with 2 tablespoons of the vinegar, 2 tablespoons of the fish sauce, and the green garlic juice. Put the eggplant in another bowl, add the remaining ¼ cup (60 ml) vinegar and 1 tablespoon fish sauce, 1 tablespoon of the olive oil, and the marjoram, and toss gently. Let marinate for 20 to 30 minutes, then drain.

When you're ready to cook the steak, heat a large carbon-steel or cast-iron skillet over medium-high heat for about 5 minutes. Add the remaining 1 tablespoon olive oil to the pan, then add the steaks, gently pressing them down to get even contact and a good sear, and let cook for 2 minutes. (You'll have to do this in two batches if your pan isn't big enough; or use two pans.) Lacquer each piece with two or three brushes of the fish sauce mixture, then flip. Cook on the second side for 2 minutes, then lacquer with more fish sauce and flip again. After a minute, lacquer with more fish sauce and flip. Cook for another minute, brush again, and flip. If you have an instant-read thermometer, use it to test your steaks' internal temperature; it should be about 125°F (52°C). If you don't have a thermometer, a cake tester inserted into the interior of the steak for 10 seconds should come out warm. When the steaks are done, let them rest for 5 minutes, ideally propped up on something—like chopsticks laid over a plate—to keep the bottoms from steaming. Set the pan aside.

While the steaks rest, gently warm the Taleggio sauce. Heat the drained leeks and eggplant on a baking sheet in a low oven or under the broiler for a minute or two, just until they're warm. Drizzle the leeks with a bit of olive oil.

Just before serving, heat the same skillet over medium heat and lightly sear the steaks again to warm them up, about 30 seconds on each side. Remove from the pan and slice each steak horizontally in half into 2 planks. Coat each seared side with a generous ½ teaspoon of the salsa verde.

To serve, spoon 1 tablespoon of the Taleggio sauce onto each of four plates, then place 2 steak slices, pink side up, on each plate. Lay an anchovy fillet on each piece of steak, then arrange the eggplant and leeks over and around the meat.

Steak with Potato Chips, Taleggio, and Spicy Marmalade

Who doesn't love a good burger? Yet I've always grappled with the idea of serving one at Estela, because you can get a really good one pretty much anywhere in New York. I settled on this recipe as a way of hitting the same notes, with steak instead of a patty, a runny Taleggio sauce in place of a slice of cheese, and a spicy marmalade standing in for the ketchup—all cloaked in an addictive veil of potato chips.

Serves 4

2 pounds (900 g) hanger steak, tough
    sinew removed, cut into 4 portions
    (ask your butcher to do this)
Kosher salt
2 garlic cloves
2 tablespoons roughly chopped rosemary
3 tablespoons extra-virgin olive oil
¼ cup (60 ml) fish sauce
¼ cup (60 ml) Taleggio Sauce (page 37)
About 1½ tablespoons Marjoram-
    Anchovy Salsa Verde (page 42)
Spicy Marmalade (page 38) or Tomato
    Chutney (page 42)
Potato Chips (page 52)
Dusting of pimentón dulce

Let your steak come to room temperature, about 30 minutes.

Coat all the pieces of steak with a generous layer of salt on all sides, really patting it into the flesh. Let sit for another 30 minutes. It may look as if it's beginning to dry out, and that's a good thing; it means you'll get a better sear.

When you're ready to cook the steak, make the garlic oil: Halve the garlic cloves, and, using a mortar and pestle, mash them with the rosemary until you have pulpy strips. Stir in 2 tablespoons of the olive oil and set aside.

Heat a large carbon-steel or cast-iron skillet over medium-high heat for about 5 minutes. Add the remaining 1 tablespoon olive oil to the pan, then add the steaks, gently pressing them down to get even contact and a good sear, and let cook for 2 minutes. (You will have to do this in batches if your pan isn't big enough; or use two pans.) Lacquer each piece with two or three brushes of fish sauce, then flip. Sear on the second side for 2 minutes, lacquer with fish sauce, and flip again. After a minute, brush on a thin layer of the garlic oil and flip. Cook for another minute, brush with garlic oil, and flip. If you have an instant-read thermometer, use it to test your steaks' internal temperature; it should be about 125°F (52°C). If you don't have a thermometer, a cake tester inserted into the interior of the steak for 10 seconds should come out warm. When the steaks are done, let them rest for 5 minutes, ideally propped up on something—like chopsticks laid over a plate—to keep the bottoms from steaming. Set the pan aside.

While the steak is resting, gently warm the Taleggio sauce.

Just before serving, heat the same skillet over medium heat and lightly sear the steaks again to warm them up, about 30 seconds on each side. Remove from the heat and spread each side of each steak with a generous ½ teaspoon of the salsa verde, then slice each steak horizontally in half into 2 planks.

To serve, spoon 1 tablespoon of the Taleggio sauce onto each of four plates, then place 2 steak slices, pink side up, on each plate. Spoon a tablespoon of the marmalade in between each pair of slices and cover each plate with a generous layer of potato chips. Add a dusting of pimentón dulce. Don't be surprised if people end up dipping their chips into the cheese sauce; it's not a bad idea.

Steak with Black Sesame Béarnaise and Turnips

A béarnaise made of a rich and nutty black sesame seed paste takes this dish to somewhere between Japan and the Middle East. We get the paste from the Japanese market, but we could just as easily reach for black tahini.

Serves 4

For the Chile Paste
2 medium-hot red chiles, such as Cherry Bomb, seeded and roughly chopped
Kosher salt
1 teaspoon grated lemon zest
1 tablespoon fresh lemon juice
2 tablespoons extra-virgin olive oil

For the Turnips
Kosher salt
4 Japanese turnips (such as hakurei or Tokyo), scrubbed clean and trimmed
2 purple-top turnips, scrubbed clean and trimmed
1 tablespoon chardonnay vinegar
1 teaspoon grated lemon zest

For the Steak
2 pounds (900 g) hanger steak, tough sinew removed, cut into 4 portions (ask your butcher to do this)
Kosher salt and ground pepper
2 garlic cloves
3 tablespoons white soy sauce (shiro shoyu)
1 tablespoon fish sauce
2 tablespoons olive oil

For the Black Sesame Béarnaise
Generous 1 tablespoon white wine, such as pinot grigio
¼ small shallot, thinly sliced
1 large egg yolk
Kosher salt
4 tablespoons (115 g) unsalted butter, melted
2¼ teaspoons black sesame paste
½ teaspoon activated charcoal powder (optional)
Cabernet vinegar

4 anchovy fillets
Gray salt and black pepper
Extra-virgin olive oil

Make the chile paste:
Using a mortar and pestle, pound the chiles until they become a rough paste—add a pinch of kosher salt to help this along too. Stir in the lemon zest and juice, then add the olive oil and stir to combine.

Make the turnips:
Bring a small pot of lightly salted water to a boil. Meanwhile, halve the Japanese turnips lengthwise, then cut into ¼-inch wedges. Move them to the side of your cutting board, keeping the pieces in order. Cut the purple-top turnips into ¼-inch-thick, bite-size pieces. Combine the vinegar, a pinch of salt, and the lemon zest in a medium bowl.

Add the purple-top turnips to the boiling water and let simmer until just warmed through, about 30 seconds. Drain, add the warmed turnips to the vinegar mixture, and toss gently to coat. (The Japanese turnips remain uncooked.)

Make the steak:
Let the steaks come to room temperature, about 30 minutes. Coat all the pieces with a generous layer of kosher salt and black pepper, really patting it into the flesh. Halve the garlic cloves and, using a mortar and pestle, mash them until you have pulpy strips. Transfer to a small bowl and stir in the white soy sauce, fish sauce, and 1 tablespoon of the olive oil.

Heat the remaining 1 tablespoon olive oil in a large carbon-steel or cast-iron skillet over medium heat, then add the steaks. (You will have to do this in batches if your pan isn't big enough; or use two pans.) Cook, flipping regularly and lacquering with two or three brushes of the white soy mixture between each flip, until a pale brown crust starts to develop and the internal temperature is about 125°F (52°C), about 4 minutes. If you don't have a meat thermometer, a cake tester inserted into the interior of the steak for 10 seconds should come out warm. When the steaks are done, let them rest for 10 minutes, ideally propped up on something—like chopsticks laid over a plate—to keep the bottoms from steaming. Set the pan aside.

continued

Make the béarnaise:

While the steak rests, combine the wine and shallot in a small saucepan and simmer over medium heat until the wine has reduced by half. Strain the reduction into a deep bowl and cool slightly.

Add the egg yolk to the reduced wine, season with kosher salt, and combine with an immersion blender or whisk. Slowly drizzle in the hot melted butter, blending or whisking constantly, until the sauce is emulsified and thickened. Stir in the black sesame paste and the activated charcoal powder, if using. Season to taste with cabernet vinegar and kosher salt, and, if necessary, thin the sauce with a few dashes of water. Set the bowl in a larger bowl of warm water to keep warm.

Just before serving, heat the steak skillet over medium heat and lightly sear the steaks again to warm them up, about 30 seconds on each side. Remove from the heat and rub each steak with some of the chile paste. Slice each steak horizontally in half into 2 planks.

To serve, set a pair of steak slices on each of four plates, cut side up. Shingle the Japanese turnips over one piece of steak, then line up the purple-top turnips alongside both pieces.

Lay an anchovy fillet over the meat and turnips. Lightly season the meat with gray salt and pepper, and finish with a drizzle of extra-virgin olive oil. Spoon a generous dollop of black sesame béarnaise onto each plate.

Veal Sweetbreads with Onion

Of all the cuts that would make it onto the grill during Sunday *asados* in Uruguay—and there were many—it's the sweetbreads I remember most fondly. While most European preparations emphasize their creaminess, usually through blanching and pan-roasting, I find that sweetbreads are far better cooked this way, with a crust and served with lemon, salt, and some gently marinated onions.

Make the onions:

Heat a small skillet over medium heat for 5 minutes. Place the onion quarters, cut side down, in the dry pan and cook for 4 minutes, or until evenly charred. Turn the onions and cook for 4 more minutes. Flip the onions so the skin side is down and cook for 6 to 8 minutes, until cooked through; when you pull them apart, each "petal" should be translucent. Cut off the root ends and separate the petals. Put them in a bowl and dress them with the vinegar and fish sauce.

Prepare the sweetbreads:

Set up an ice bath. Cut the sweetbreads into 2 equal pieces. Put them in a pot of lightly salted water to cover and bring to a simmer, then transfer the blanched sweetbreads, with their cooking water, to a bowl and set it in the ice bath to cool.

Meanwhile, using a mortar and pestle, crush the garlic into tiny chunks, but not to a paste. Add the rosemary and pound together with the garlic to release the herb's oils. Add the fish sauce.

Remove the cooled sweetbreads from the water, transfer to a cutting board, and pat dry. Score on both sides with a sharp knife in a crisscross pattern, cutting about ¼ inch into the sweetbreads to ensure even cooking and some crisp bits.

Heat a large skillet over medium-high heat, then add 1 teaspoon of the olive oil and let it heat up. Add the sweetbreads and let them cook, undisturbed, for a few minutes to start a good sear. Then begin to lacquer them with the fish sauce mixture. Flip once you get a nice deep golden color on the first side, with a few charred bits, and continue to lacquer them and deglaze the pan with the fish sauce as you finish cooking, making sure to sear them on all sides; total cooking time should be 10 to 12 minutes. Remove from the heat.

While the sweetbreads cook, rewarm the onions briefly under the broiler or in a low oven. To serve, arrange the sweetbreads on two plates with the onion. Give each serving a good squeeze of lemon and drizzle with the remaining olive oil.

Serves 2

For the Onions
½ Spanish onion, not peeled, root end trimmed but left in place, cut in half
1 tablespoon sherry vinegar
1 tablespoon fish sauce

For the Sweetbreads
8 to 10 ounces (about 260 g) veal sweetbreads
Kosher salt
2 garlic cloves
2 teaspoons finely minced rosemary
3 tablespoons fish sauce
2 teaspoons extra-virgin olive oil

2 lemon wedges

This dish is based on the best sweetbreads I've ever
had, which chef and dear friend Santiago Garat
made for me one summer in Buenos Aires.

Houston Street Asado

For an *asado* to be a success, there's actually not much to it, even though there will always be some uncertainty, no matter how many times you have done it before. I quite like that. A few loose guidelines follow. Just remember to be cautious, though there isn't much to fear.

Try to have some snacks—oysters, prosciutto, olives—ready before you cook, so no one feels rushed. You could maybe get some sausages and grill and slice them as you go, or you could do sweetbreads. You want to build anticipation, for people to wait for the steak.

As I suggested, there is no set way to do it. And you don't need anything fancy: a simple Weber grill, sometimes just a griddle set on a few stones is sufficient, depending on your surroundings. The specific charcoal is to me the most important thing to source. We tend to use natural Japanese charcoal. Not out of a snobbishness but because commercial varieties tend to impart a synthetic taste. Quality charcoal will also hold the heat more evenly.

Ensure that you have the right tools: some tongs, some dry rags, a long-reaching spatula to move the coals, a little water in case something catches on fire.

Season your meat with a generous—and I mean generous—amount of salt and pepper. I find meat without salt just flat, boring protein. It becomes meat when it is properly seasoned.

Ensure that your griddle is clean. I like to do this with an oily cloth or rag. To light your charcoal or fire, there are many YouTube videos that can help you much more effectively than I can. What I will say is that you always want to have enough charcoal on hand, so keep some extra aside, in case you need it.

Once your charcoal is ready, distribute it evenly. I like to casually create different temperature areas so that I can move the meat around if it is cooking too fast, and vice versa. This is important with these rib eyes, whose fat tends to render and create flame. You don't want that charred effect, that flavor of combustion.

Even if you have no idea what you are doing, be confident. Remember that this is the most basic form of cooking. The key is determining the right temperature, which can be tricky. These days, there are digital thermometers, but I prefer not to use them. Instead, hold your hand over the grill flush with the top edge of the steak. You want to be able to count up to 5 or 6 seconds before it gets so hot that you have to remove your hand. This indicates medium to low heat, what you want for a thicker cut of rib eye.

I like to start with the bone side down to ensure that all the meat and fat between the ribs gets properly rendered. It really is the best part. Again, a reminder that you can always move your meat to hotter areas if it feels as if it is going too slow—or too fast. You can also raise the temperature by moving or fanning the charcoal. You will likely find yourself making adjustments throughout the process, which is fine. Try to keep in mind that you want it to go fairly slowly and that there is no rush: between lighting the fire, cleaning the grill, and setting everything up, the entire process will take about two hours.

When is the meat done? You can tell by the way it looks but also by touching. If it's too soft, there's too much give, that means it's too rare. If it looks done on the outside and feels too soft, you probably rushed it, so you can put it back on "a slow area" of the grill to let it cook through. A lot of purists will question what I am about to tell you, but I don't see why you can't split it open and finish cooking it that way, if it's easier for you.

What to eat with it: Have some preboiled potatoes on hand to make a potato salad. You could even cook them wrapped in aluminum foil over the coals. In either case, peel them, crush them by hand, and add a good amount of mayonnaise, a good amount of salt, a splash of olive oil, and cracked black pepper. You could add a dash of mustard or vinegar if you feel like it, but I prefer to keep it rich.

Preslice some cherry tomatoes and onions. Right before the steaks are done, add salt, vinegar, olive oil, onions, basil, and parsley. In this case, I like the tomatoes to have enough acidity, so I introduce some lemon zest and lemon juice.

Finally, you can do a marjoram and anchovy salsa verde or a traditional chimichurri. I am also a fan of Dijon mustard. Try some pieces of steak alone, some with Dijon, some with Dijon and salsa verde, however you like.

And if at any time you feel like some of the pieces need to be cooked more, throw them back on the grill.

brunch

All these dishes are pretty much as indulgent as it gets without going too far. You'll encounter classic reference points throughout, like a dish of eggs and harissa that to me feels like huevos rancheros and a sandwich that pays tribute to the corner deli by my house. But even the grilled cucumber, which may seem unusual in any part of a menu, to me is just as good as, if not better than, any breakfast sausage.

Toast with Lardo and Jam

You don't need to be a good cook or a cook at all to make good toast; you just need to be hungry. But when you're starved, you tend to take shortcuts. It sometimes helps to calm down and proceed with care. That is the case here, with a toast that glistens in a way that's almost improper.

Practical Note: You want a jam that has some chunkiness to it, with good acidity to play off the fat. I like rhubarb or plum, or even pineapple, here. (Note that the fruit must macerate overnight before you make the jam.)

Heat a large carbon-steel or cast-iron skillet over medium-high heat. Brush each slice of bread lightly with olive oil, set it in the hot pan, and toast, turning once, until well charred on both sides.

Rub the hot toasts with the garlic, using a very light hand—you just want to perfume the bread, without raking the garlic into it. Spread the toasts thickly with the jam and sprinkle with the lemon zest.

Return the pan to medium-high heat while you drape the toasts with the lardo, ruffling the lardo very slightly so it looks rumpled rather than flat on the toasts. Set the toasts in the hot pan, cover, and heat just until the lardo is shiny and beginning to turn translucent, about a minute. Sprinkle the toasts with gray salt and serve immediately.

Serves 4

**Four 1-inch-thick slices miche,
  cut from the widest part of the loaf
Extra-virgin olive oil
1 garlic clove
½ cup (100 g) Rhubarb or Plum Jam
  (recipe follows)
Grated zest of ½ lemon
4 ounces (115 g) lardo, very thinly sliced
Gray salt**

Rhubarb or Plum Jam

Stir together the fruit and sugar in a large bowl. Cover with plastic wrap and let macerate overnight in the refrigerator.

The next day, put a small plate or saucer in the freezer. Transfer the fruit and all its juices to a large saucepan, bring to a boil, and boil to reduce by about half, 10 to 15 minutes, stirring occasionally to prevent scorching the jam. When the jam has thickened, drop a small spoonful onto the cold saucer. If it has set and wrinkles when you touch it, the jam is ready; if not, continue to boil until it does.

Remove from the heat and season with citric acid, pinch by pinch, to taste. Let cool, then transfer to a large jar or other container, cover, and refrigerate.

Makes 3 cups

**2 pounds (900 g) rhubarb, trimmed and
  coarsely chopped, or plums, halved,
  pitted, and coarsely chopped
2¼ cups (425 g) sugar
Citric acid (or substitute fresh lemon
  juice)**

A sunny-side up egg with a slab of beer-soaked bacon (see page 240) and Toast with Lardo and Jam

Slab Bacon with Dijon, Potato, and Egg

A classic pairing, eggs and bacon, done our way. We lacquer the thick slab bacon with a savory and complex dark beer glaze as it cooks.

Practical Note: Get the bacon from a good butcher; you need whole chunks, not slices. We like Nueske's.

Bring a medium saucepan of water to a boil over high heat. Salt the water generously, add the potatoes and bay leaves, and boil for 12 to 15 minutes, until the potatoes are tender. Drain and set aside.

Heat a large carbon-steel or cast-iron skillet over medium heat until hot. Add the bacon and cook, brushing it regularly with a thin layer of glaze to flavor and lacquer it and turning the pieces every few minutes to brown them on all sides. This will take about 15 minutes; be patient—the bacon should be shiny and well browned, and most of the fat should be rendered. Transfer the pieces of bacon to a paper towel–lined plate and brush on all sides with the garlic oil; reserve the rendered fat.

Put the potatoes and a few tablespoons of the bacon fat in a skillet and warm over low heat, turning the potatoes occasionally.

Set a large nonstick skillet over medium heat and film it with a little olive oil. Add the eggs and fry sunny-side up; you want the whites to be just set, with no crisp or browned parts.

To serve, divide the warm potatoes among four plates and put a piece of bacon on each plate. Carefully drape the fried eggs over the potatoes, garnish each plate with a dollop of Dijon mustard, and sprinkle the eggs with gray salt.

Serves 4

Kosher salt
12 ounces (340 g) small Golden Nugget or
    other creamy potatoes, scrubbed
2 bay leaves
Four thick 3½-ounce (100 g) slices slab
    bacon, about 1½ inches wide, top skin
    left on
Dark Beer Glaze (recipe follows)
¼ cup (60 ml) Garlic Oil (page 46)
Extra-virgin olive oil
4 large eggs
4 heaping teaspoons Dijon mustard
Gray salt

Dark Beer Glaze

Bring the beer to a boil in a medium saucepan over high heat, then reduce the heat to medium-high and boil until the beer has reduced to 1 cup, 25 to 30 minutes; be careful not to let the beer boil over. Remove from the heat and whisk in the mustard, miso, and soy sauce. Use immediately, or transfer to a container, let cool, and refrigerate for up to 4 days.

Makes 1½ cups

1½ cups (360 ml) dark beer
¾ cup (175 g) Dijon mustard
¼ cup (50 g) yellow miso or similar
    light miso
1½ tablespoons white soy sauce
    (shiro shoyu)

Tomatoes with Fromager d'Affinois on Toast

You should definitely try this in the summer, when tomatoes are abundant and at their peak. You want them on the riper side, and as you will see, you'll want quite a bit of them.

Serves 1; easily multiplied

1 rectangular loaf pumpernickel or other dense, seeded bread (you'll have plenty left over)
About 2 teaspoons extra-virgin olive oil
1 garlic clove
Generous 2 tablespoons softened Fromager d'Affinois or other triple-cream French cheese, such as Brie (with or without rind, as desired)
1 firm but ripe heirloom tomato, sliced into ⅛-inch-thick rounds
Kosher salt
Gray salt

Lay the loaf of bread on one end and slice off the bottom crust with a bread knife and discard. Then slice a plank, about ⅛ inch thick, off the bottom (this is what you'll use for the toast). It's easiest to do this by standing the loaf up on end and slicing down into it to start, then laying the loaf down once you're an inch or so in, so the slice doesn't break, and continuing to cut the bread. (Try to get it as even as possible, but don't stress about it too much.) Cut off the crusts from this slice.

Heat a large carbon-steel or cast-iron skillet over medium-high heat and add about 1 teaspoon of the olive oil. Add the slice of bread and toast it on both sides, pressing down on the bread with the back of a spatula so it cooks evenly, until you have a good char and most of the surface of the bread is a nice deep brown, about 5 minutes. It's okay to have a few blackened bits; if the edges are burnt, just slice them off.

Rub one side of the warm toast lightly with the garlic, then smear on the cheese in a light, even layer. Lay the sliced tomato out on the cutting board and sprinkle with a pinch of kosher salt and then with a small pinch of gray salt for texture. Arrange them on the toast, letting them drape over the sides. Give it all a light drizzle of the remaining olive oil. Eat with a fork and knife.

English Muffins with Smoked Whitefish and Trout Roe

A way to honor a neighbor, Russ & Daughters, who will ship the whitefish for this sandwich from their iconic Houston Street shop to your home (see Sourcing, page 296). While you should leave that part to them, try to make your own muffins.

Practical Notes: Smoked whitefish varies in how moist it is, so you may need to add more crème fraîche to the mix if yours is on the drier side.

If ramps are out of season, you can substitute any fragrant allium— spring onions, green garlic, shallots, scallions, or even very finely sliced Spanish onion.

Note that you will need to start the muffin recipe 2 days ahead.

Make the whitefish mixture:
Combine the crème fraîche, cream cheese, and pickled ramps in a small bowl. Gently fold in the smoked whitefish. Season with a splash of the ramp pickling liquid, then taste again and adjust the seasoning. If the mix seems dry, add a little more crème fraîche and stir to combine.

To serve, soak the sliced onions in a bowl of ice water while you preheat the broiler, then drain and pat dry.

Halve the English muffins and toast under the broiler until lightly charred. Spread both cut sides of the muffins with the aioli. Top the bottom halves with the whitefish mixture. Top each one with 6 or 7 onion rings and dollop evenly with the trout roe. Close the sandwiches with the muffin tops and serve.

Serves 4

For the Whitefish Mixture
1 tablespoon plus 1 teaspoon crème fraîche, or as needed
1 tablespoon plus 2 teaspoons cream cheese
2 generous tablespoons thinly sliced Pickled Ramp whites (page 295, or see Notes), plus pickling liquid to taste
7 ounces (200 g) smoked whitefish, broken into large flakes

1 Spanish onion, sliced into scant ¼-inch-thick rings
4 English Muffins (recipe follows)
2 tablespoons Aioli (page 49)
2 tablespoons trout roe

English Muffins

Two days before you plan to cook the muffins, make the starter:
Combine the flour, water, and yeast in a medium bowl, cover with plastic wrap or a damp kitchen towel, and let ferment overnight at room temperature.

The next day, make the levain and secondary mixes:
To make the levain, stir together the flour and yeast in a large bowl, then add the starter and water and stir until thoroughly combined. To make the secondary mix, stir together the flour and salt in another large bowl, then add the water and stir until thoroughly combined; the mixture will seem relatively dry.

Cover both mixtures with plastic wrap or damp kitchen towels and let rise for 90 minutes, or until the levain is bubbling.

Add the secondary mix to the levain and knead lightly to blend well. Cover and let rise overnight in the refrigerator.

Make the rolling mix:
Grind the rice in a blender, mini food processor, or spice grinder until fine; the consistency should be like coarse cornmeal. Do the same with the oats, then combine the two in a bowl and set aside.

The next day, when you are ready to make the muffins, dust a work surface with about one-third of the rolling mix. Remove the dough from the refrigerator, punch it down lightly, and transfer to the work surface. With a floured rolling pin, roll the dough out into a rough rectangle about a generous inch thick. Dust the surface of the dough with another third of the rolling mix. Use a 3-inch biscuit cutter or ring mold to cut out the muffins and place them on a floured baking sheet. (You can reroll the scraps to make more muffins: knead together gently and roll out, using the remaining rolling mix.) Cover with a damp kitchen towel and let proof for 10 to 15 minutes, until risen by about half.

Heat a large carbon-steel or cast-iron skillet or a griddle over medium-low heat until hot and brush generously with clarified butter. Cook the muffins in batches, turning once, for 10 to 12 minutes on each side, until the tops and bottoms are well browned and the muffins are cooked through. (A thermometer inserted into the center of one should register between 190° and 200°F/93° and 100°C.) Transfer to a wire rack to cool.

The muffins can be stored in an airtight container at room temperature for a day or so; they can also be frozen in a heavy-duty zip-top bag for up to 3 months.

Makes 12 to 14 muffins

For the Starter
1⅓ cups (195 g) all-purpose flour
¾ cup (180 ml) plus 1 tablespoon warm water
2 teaspoons active dry yeast

For the Levain Mix
1 cup (145 g) plus 1 tablespoon all-purpose flour
1 teaspoon active dry yeast
Scant 7 ounces (about 200 g) starter (half the starter)
⅔ cup (160 ml) plus 2 teaspoons warm water

For the Secondary Mix
6¾ cups (980 g) plus 1 tablespoon all-purpose flour
3 tablespoons plus 1 teaspoon kosher salt
2⅓ cups (560 ml) water

For the Rolling Mix
½ cup (95 g) brown rice
½ cup (60 g) rolled oats

Clarified butter, melted, for cooking the muffins

English Muffin with Smoked Whitefish and Trout Roe (*left*) and Egg, Pancetta, and Avocado Sandwich (page 248)

Egg, Pancetta, and Avocado Sandwich

Though every bacon, egg, and cheese sandwich satisfies, here's one of the best (without cheese). We use *tebirke*, which is a Danish pastry with nice notes of sweetness from the frangipane (almond pastry cream). If you can't find it, try using brioche. It's hard to go wrong.

Use a sturdy whisk to mash the avocado flesh into a mostly smooth paste in a medium bowl. Season with the lemon juice and salt and set aside.

Preheat the broiler. Slice each tebirke horizontally in half and set on a baking sheet, cut sides up. Put the pancetta on the same baking sheet and slide under the broiler. Remove the tebirke when they are lightly toasted, about 45 seconds, and continue to broil the pancetta, turning once, until it has crisped at the edges but is still flexible, about 5 minutes in all. Remove from the heat.

Meanwhile, film a medium nonstick skillet with a little olive oil and set over medium-low heat. Crack the eggs into the pan and fry very gently until the whites are just set. Turn the heat to low, cover the pan, and cook for about 40 seconds, just until a white film begins to appear over the yolks. (This will keep the yolks from bursting when you close the sandwiches.) Remove from the heat.

Brush the bottom halves of the toasted tebirkes with some of the fat the pancetta has rendered, then spread one-quarter of the avocado mash onto each one. Dollop evenly with the aioli and season generously with a squiggle of Sriracha over the aioli. Top with the crisped pancetta.

Carefully transfer the eggs to the bottoms of the tebirkes, folding the white of each egg slightly under itself so it fits neatly on the pastry. Close the sandwiches with the top halves of the tebirke and serve immediately. **PICTURED ON PAGE 247.**

Serves 4

3 ripe avocados, halved, pitted, and
    peeled
Juice of ½ lemon
2 teaspoons kosher salt
4 tebirkes or almond croissants
4 ounces (115 g) very thinly sliced
    pancetta
Extra-virgin olive oil
4 large eggs
1 tablespoon plus 1 teaspoon Aioli
    (page 49)
Sriracha

Grilled Cucumbers with Béarnaise and Herb Salad

This recipe proves those of us who expect cucumbers to be boring and dull completely wrong. Find out for yourself.

Practical Notes: Look for denser and, most important, less watery cucumbers that will hold their shape rather than collapsing when grilled. Note that the cucumbers are first charred, then marinated overnight, and then grilled.

At the restaurant, we make this with a vegan XO sauce and bonji, a condiment made from fermented rye berries that is similar to soy sauce (both sourced from Momofuku Lab). You can substitute our XO sauce (see the recipe on page 45, or use a good supermarket brand) for the vegan XO and soy sauce for the bonji.

Char the cucumbers over a gas flame or on a grill, turning occasionally, just until beginning to char. Remove from the heat and let cool slightly.

Make the marinade:
Combine the XO sauce, soy sauce, sesame oil, grapeseed oil, bonji, and garlic in a bowl.

Use a knife to very lightly score the cucumbers, as you would a piece of meat, and put them in a quart-size zip-top plastic bag. Pour in the marinade, seal the bag, and marinate the cucumbers overnight in the refrigerator.

Make the béarnaise:
The next day, just before grilling the cucumbers, combine the wine and shallot in a small saucepan and simmer over medium heat until the wine is reduced by half. Strain the reduction into a deep bowl and let cool slightly. Discard the shallot.

Add the egg yolk to the reduced wine, season with the salt, and combine with an immersion blender or whisk. Slowly drizzle in the hot melted butter, blending or whisking constantly, until the sauce is emulsified and thickened. Set the bowl in a larger bowl of warm water to keep the sauce warm.

Grill the cucumbers over a gas flame or on a hot grill, turning occasionally, just until charred on all sides and warm inside but not cooked through.

continued

Serves 4

4 small Vertina cucumbers, or other small dense cucumbers
4 small white or green Kirby cucumbers

For the Marinade
¼ cup (60 ml) plus 2 tablespoons vegan XO sauce (see Notes)
5 teaspoons white soy sauce (shiro shoyu)
2 teaspoons toasted sesame oil
4 teaspoons grapeseed oil
5 teaspoons bonji or soy sauce (see Notes)
1 garlic clove, grated

For the Béarnaise Sauce
Generous 1 tablespoon white wine, such as pinot grigio
¼ small shallot, thinly sliced
1 large egg yolk
Pinch of kosher salt, or to taste
4 tablespoons (115 g) unsalted butter, melted and still hot

A large handful of mild but aromatic tender leaves (about 24 leaves), such as anise hyssop, shiso, Egyptian spinach, or wild spinach
Juice of ½ lemon

Clockwise from top left: Grilled Cucumbers with Béarnaise and Herb Salad; Eggs with Beans, Harissa, and Mojama (page 253); our blood cake, breaded and served with eggs in a sandwich (see page 256)

Spoon about 2 tablespoons of the warm béarnaise into a circle in the center of each of four plates (you will have some béarnaise left over, but it's difficult to make a smaller amount; it's a little extra treat). Set a Vertina cucumber just to the side of the béarnaise on each plate. Cut the Kirby cucumbers into 1-inch-thick slices and lay them on the opposite side of the béarnaise.

Toss the tender leaves with the lemon juice and arrange one-quarter of them, overlapping slightly, over the sliced cucumbers on each plate and serve.

Eggs with Beans, "Harissa," and Mojama

I could tell you a lot about the great ingredients that go into this dish, but at the end of the day, these are my huevos rancheros, amigos.

Serves 6

1 ounce (30 g) mojama
   (see Estela Essentials, page 30)
1 pound (450 g) dried corona beans
2 bay leaves
1 Spanish onion, halved
1 tablespoon kosher salt, or to taste

For the Bread Crumbs
1 garlic clove
Gray salt
1 tablespoon extra-virgin olive oil
¾ cup (30 g) torn ½-inch pieces day-
   old sourdough bread (you want a few
   pieces with some dark crust)

For the Herb Salad
A large handful of cilantro leaves
½ Spanish onion, sliced as thin as
   possible, soaked in ice water for
   30 minutes, and drained
Grated zest and juice of 1 lemon

Extra-virgin olive oil
12 large eggs
¾ cup Harissa (recipe follows)
2 tablespoons crème fraîche
Gray salt
Chile flakes
Arbequina olive oil

Practical Notes: You can substitute other dried white beans for the coronas, but you may need to reduce the cooking time—coronas are very large and need more time than most white beans.

The mojama (salt-cured tuna) needs to dry for 48 hours before you make this recipe.

Harissa is lovely with roasted fish or chicken. I like it in a grilled cheese sandwich or with blood cake (see page 257).

You'll need to dry the mojama to a point where you can shave it: Wrap it in cheesecloth, secure it with kitchen string, and suspend it from a cabinet door or other out-of-the-way place, at room temperature, for 48 hours. To test it, shave off a small piece using a vegetable peeler or mandoline; the mojama should be crisp-chewy and dry. Wrap tightly in plastic wrap and refrigerate until you're ready to use it.

Meanwhile, put the beans in a large pot, cover with 3 inches of cool water, and soak overnight.

The next day, drain the beans, then return them to the pot, cover with 3 inches of fresh water, and add the bay leaves and halved onion. Bring to a boil over high heat, then reduce the heat to medium, partially cover, and simmer very gently until the beans are tender, about 3 hours. Stir in the salt, taste, and adjust the seasoning if necessary. Let the beans cool completely in their liquid, then cover and refrigerate. (The beans can be cooked up to a day ahead.)

Make the bread crumbs:
Preheat the oven to 375°F (190°C).

Using a mortar and pestle, mash the garlic with a pinch of gray salt until wispy. Stir in the olive oil. Put the torn bread on a baking sheet and toss with the garlic oil. Spread out on the pan and toast, tossing the bread every few minutes, until it is browned and crisp but not hard, 4 to 5 minutes. Remove from the oven and set aside.

continued

Just before serving, make the salad:

Gently toss the cilantro and onion with the lemon zest and juice in a small bowl.

To cook the eggs, film two large nonstick skillets with a little olive oil and heat over medium-low heat until hot. Gently crack 6 eggs into each pan (their whites will become one, which is fine) and cook until the whites are cooked but not browned or crisped at all.

While the eggs cook, warm the harissa in a medium saucepan. Fold in the bread crumbs, stirring to coat, then divide among six bowls.

Wipe out the pan and add the beans and a splash of their liquid. Warm through, then spoon the beans over the harissa. Top each bowl of beans with a teaspoon of crème fraîche, then arrange the salad on top of that.

Use a spatula to divide each pan of eggs into 3 portions (2 eggs each) and drape one portion over each bowl of salad. Shave the mojama into petals on a mandoline and scatter over the eggs. Sprinkle each bowl with gray salt, chile flakes, and a drizzle of Arbequina olive oil and serve.

"Harissa"

Heat the olive oil in a large saucepan over medium-low heat. Add the onion and sweat until just becoming soft and translucent, 7 to 10 minutes, then add the garlic and cook until fragrant, about 1 minute. Add the tomato, with its juice, and crush it with a wooden spoon. Cook until slightly thickened and bubbling, about 3 minutes.

Meanwhile, thinly slice the red peppers and chop them very roughly to get short, thin strips. Add them, along with the harissa, sugar, and salt, to the tomato-onion mixture and cook, stirring, until thickened and bubbling, 3 to 4 minutes. Splash in a bit of sherry vinegar and stir well to combine, then taste and adjust the seasoning as necessary.

Remove from the heat and let cool. The mixture will keep, covered, in the refrigerator for up to a week.

Makes about 1¾ cups

1 tablespoon extra-virgin olive oil
¼ Spanish onion, thinly sliced
1 small garlic clove, sliced
1 canned whole tomato, plus
    2 tablespoons of its juice
4 red bell peppers, roasted, peeled,
    and seeded
½ cup (110 g) harissa, preferably
    Mina brand
½ teaspoon sugar
1 teaspoon kosher salt
Sherry vinegar

Sam Lawrence, one of our chefs de cuisine

Blood Cake with Fried Eggs

This may intimidate at first—that was certainly the case for me as a child, when I had to stir the blood from the slain pig to help out on the farm. But there's really no difference between eating any piece of meat, a hot dog, and a truly delicious blood cake, like this one. That said, this is probably for the most adventurous among you, a weekend project. But there's plenty you can do with the result aside from serving it with eggs: bread, fry, and put it in a sandwich. Or, if you like, use it for a Thanksgiving stuffing.

Practical Notes: To get the blood and head, call up a good butcher. Failing that, Asian markets usually have blood in stock.

Put the aioli in a small cup and season with a few rasps of lemon zest. Halve the lemon and add a squeeze of juice to the aioli.

Heat a large carbon-steel or cast-iron skillet over medium-high heat, then add 1 tablespoon of the olive oil. Add 3 slices of blood cake and sear for a minute or so on each side, until crisp. Transfer to a platter and repeat with the remaining slices, adding more oil to the pan if necessary. Cover the platter with foil to keep warm, or keep warm in a low oven.

To cook the eggs, film a large nonstick skillet with olive oil and heat over medium-low heat. Crack in the eggs, season with salt, and cook the eggs gently until the whites are just set. (You can cover the pan, if you like, for quicker results.)

Arrange each slice of blood cake on a plate and top with a dollop of the seasoned aioli and a pinch of parsley. Lay the eggs on top and serve.

Serves 6

4 tablespoons Aioli (page 49)
1 lemon
About 3 tablespoons extra-virgin olive oil
Six ½-inch-thick slices Blood Cake
    (recipe follows)
6 large eggs
Kosher salt
Chopped parsley

Blood Cake

Makes twenty-four ½-inch-thick slices

For the Brine
3 quarts plus 1 cup (3 l) water
1 cup (100 g) kosher salt
1 pig's head (6 to 8 pounds/275 to 350 kg)

8 ounces (225 g) lardo, sliced ¼ inch
thick (if you can't get presliced lardo
from the butcher, freeze it to firm it,
then slice it)
½ cup (80 g) jasmine rice
¼ cup (60 g) duck fat
1½ cups (140 g) finely diced white onion
(about 1 large onion)
4 medium garlic cloves, minced almost
to a paste with a pinch of salt
Kosher salt
2 teaspoons freshly ground black pepper
1 teaspoon ground cinnamon
1 teaspoon ground allspice
8½ cups (2 l) pork blood,
at room temperature

Practical Notes: You only need 6 slices of the blood cake for the recipe on the opposite page; of course, you could scale up that recipe to serve more. Or brown and crisp some of the remaining slices and serve on rolls with Harissa (page 254), Tomato Chutney (page 42), or even just Dijon mustard. You can also freeze the extra slices to use in this dish at a later time or in sandwiches; thaw them in the refrigerator before using. (Leftover cake cannot be refrozen.)

To brine the pig's head, pour the water into a very large nonreactive container, add the salt, and stir to dissolve it. Add the pig's head, making sure it's fully submerged (add more water if necessary), and refrigerate for 24 hours.

The next step is boiling—you can do this a few days ahead of time and then refrigerate or freeze the meat (and the fat for the blood cake). Put the pig's head in the largest pot you have, add water to cover by 2 inches or so, and bring to a boil, then reduce the heat and simmer for 2 to 3 hours, until the meat is fork-tender. Remove from the heat and let cool.

Remove the skin from the pig's head and reserve. Remove all the meat from the head, discarding the cartilage and other undesirable bits and shred. Remove the fat and cut enough of it into ¼-inch dice to make 3 tablespoons. (Reserve the rest of the fat for other uses, such as frying potatoes.) Chop the skin into ¼-inch dice. Combine the skin, meat, and 3 tablespoons of fat in a large bowl. For this recipe, you need ¼ cup of this meat mixture; reserve the rest for another use (we freeze the extra meat mix in portions for future blood cakes). Refrigerate the meat mix if not using immediately, then bring to room temperature before proceeding.

continued

When ready to make the blood cake, put the lardo in the freezer.

Rinse the rice thoroughly in a fine-mesh sieve, put it in a small saucepan, add ½ cup water, and bring to a boil, then immediately reduce the heat to a simmer, cover, and cook for 10 minutes. Turn the heat off and let the rice sit for 10 minutes. Fluff with a fork; it should be cooked but toothsome. You need 1¼ cups (200 g) cooked rice for this recipe; transfer it to a large bowl.

Meanwhile, melt the duck fat in a large skillet over medium-low heat. Add the onion, garlic, and a pinch of salt and cook, stirring occasionally, until the onion is softened and translucent, 8 to 10 minutes. Remove from the heat and let cool.

Slice the chilled lardo into ¼-inch cubes.

Add the onion mixture, lardo, the reserved meat mixture, 4 teaspoons salt, the pepper, and the spices to the rice and mix well.

Preheat the oven to 325°F (170°C). Line a Pullman loaf pan with two layers of plastic wrap, leaving an overhang on the two long sides. Set it in a large high-sided baking pan. Have an instant-read thermometer handy.

Pour the blood into a large pot and heat, stirring constantly with a heatproof spatula in figure-8 and half-circle motions and making sure to maintain contact with the bottom of the pot so the blood does not burn, until the blood reaches 160°F (70°C); measure the temperature in different parts of the pot to get the most accurate reading. Immediately transfer the blood to the bowl with the rice mixture and quickly mix together with a whisk.

Transfer the mixture to the Pullman pan, cover it with the overhanging plastic, and place the loaf pan and baking pan in the oven. Carefully pour enough warm water into the baking pan to reach the level of the blood cake mixture. Cover the whole setup with foil and bake for 45 minutes, or until a cake tester inserted into the center of the cake comes out clean.

Let the blood cake cool, then remove it from the pan, transfer to a platter, and refrigerate until ready to serve. You need 6 slices of the blood cake for the recipe; the remaining cake can be sliced and stored in an airtight container, with layers of parchment between the slices, in the freezer for up to 3 months.

desser

I am not a big dessert person, or more accurately put, I like saying that. Like the rest of the food at the restaurant, our desserts provide unexpected comfort, and you might say there is something for everyone, including some recipes that are quite easy.

ts

You'll notice ingredients such as stabilizers that you are perhaps not used to, but this is a good opportunity to see how they work. Also, feel free to source your own sorbets and ice creams if you can't make them yourself.

Panna Cotta with Honey

Who doesn't love a good custard? This version is one of the easiest desserts to make that isn't just a bowl of fruit. What distinguishes it is the mixture of honey and cabernet vinegar on top, to cut through the creaminess and add some excitement, as well as a sprinkling of bee pollen.

Serves 6

3½ gelatin sheets
4 cups (scant 1 l) heavy cream
¼ cup (50 g) sugar
1 vanilla bean
¼ cup (60 ml) honey
2 tablespoons cabernet vinegar
Flaky salt and bee pollen, for garnish

Bloom (soften) the gelatin sheets in a bowl of cold water for 20 minutes, then squeeze the water out of them and set them aside. Prepare an ice bath.

Combine the heavy cream and sugar in a large saucepan and bring to a boil. Remove from the heat, add the gelatin sheets, and stir to dissolve. Strain the mixture into a heatproof bowl, to get rid of any wayward gelatin bits, and set the bowl in the ice bath to cool to room temperature.

Split the vanilla bean lengthwise, scrape the seeds into the panna cotta base, and mix well. Pour the mixture into six 7-ounce (200 ml) ramekins or small bowls, leaving at least ½ inch of space at the top. Cover with plastic wrap and refrigerate for at least 3 hours to set.

When ready to serve, whisk together the honey and vinegar in a small bowl until well combined. Top each ramekin with a spoonful of the mixture, then finish with a sprinkle of flaky salt and another of bee pollen.

Chocolate Pots de Crème

Layers of creamy chocolate, salty-rich streusel crumble, and whipped cream: What else do you need? You'll have leftover streusel, which is perfect sprinkled on ice cream.

Make the pots de crème:
Preheat the oven to 250°F (120°C).

Put the chopped chocolate in a heatproof bowl. Combine the heavy cream and milk in a small saucepan and bring to a boil.

Meanwhile, whisk together the egg yolks and sugar in a bowl. When the cream mixture comes to a boil, remove from the heat and, whisking constantly, add about ¼ cup (60 ml) of the cream to the egg mixture to temper it, then whisk in another ¼ cup (60 ml) of the cream. Return the mixture to the saucepan and cook over medium heat, stirring constantly with a heatproof spatula to keep the eggs from curdling, until the custard reaches 175°F (79°C). (If a few little curds appear, don't worry—you'll blend them away later.)

Pour the cream mixture over the chocolate and stir gently with the spatula until the chocolate melts. Blend with an immersion blender until smooth.

Arrange six 7-ounce (200 ml) ramekins in a baking pan that holds them comfortably and add the chocolate mixture, filling them just halfway. Add enough hot water to the pan so the water comes halfway up the sides of the ramekins and bake for 12 minutes, or until the custards are set but still slightly jiggly. Remove the pots de crème from the water bath and let cool, then refrigerate, covered, for a few hours, until the custard firms up. (The pots de crème can be made up to 1 day ahead.)

Make the streusel:
Combine the flour, spices, salt, and ground coffee in a medium bowl. In the large bowl of a stand mixer fitted with the paddle attachment, cream the butter and brown sugar together until light and fluffy (you can also use a hand mixer). Add the flour mixture and mix until well incorporated—it will be almost wet looking, like damp earth. Turn the mixture out onto a parchment-lined baking sheet or pan and press it into an even layer about ½ inch thick. Chill it in the refrigerator for 30 minutes.

Serves 6

For the Pots de Crème
5 ounces (150 g) 70% chocolate, chopped
1⅓ cups (320 ml) heavy cream
¾ cup (180 ml) milk
8 large egg yolks
¼ cup (50 g) sugar

For the Streusel
Scant 1 cup (135 g) all-purpose flour, plus more for dusting
¾ teaspoon ground cardamom
½ teaspoon ground cinnamon
¼ teaspoon kosher salt
⅓ cup (75 g) coffee beans, ground in a coffee grinder until coarse and gravelly
8 tablespoons (1 stick; 115 g) unsalted butter, at room temperature
½ cup (100 g) plus 1 tablespoon lightly packed dark brown sugar

½ cup (120 ml) heavy cream, whipped to soft peaks
Cocoa powder, for dusting

Preheat the oven to 350°F (180°C).

Break the chilled streusel into ½-inch pieces using your hands. The size of the pieces will vary, but that's okay. Dust with flour and toss to coat. (The streusel can be made ahead to this point and frozen on a small baking sheet until ready to bake.)

Spread the streusel out on a parchment-lined baking sheet in a single layer. Bake for 12 to 15 minutes, or until dry and crumbly. Remove from the oven and let cool. (The streusel will keep in an airtight container at room temperature for up to a week.)

Before serving, let the pots de crème come to room temperature (about 30 minutes). To serve, top each pot de crème with a few tablespoons of streusel, then fill the rest of the ramekin with whipped cream and level it off with the back of a knife. Dust with cocoa powder and serve.

Chocolate Cake with Whipped Cream

Broiling slices of this luscious chocolate cake before serving creates a crust similar to a crème brûlée and adds a wanted burnt-flavor note. The black sesame ganache delivers savory notes, and the whipped cream refreshes.

Serves 6

⅔ cup (175 g) Sesame Ganache
    (recipe follows)
6 squares Chocolate Cake
    (recipe follows)
Gray salt
1 cup (240 ml) heavy cream,
    whipped to soft peaks
Cocoa powder, for dusting

About an hour before serving, remove the ganache from the refrigerator to come to room temperature.

When you're ready to serve, preheat the broiler to high, with a rack as close to the flame as possible.

Arrange the pieces of cake on a baking sheet and broil for a few minutes, until they get a good char on their tops. (Depending on the strength of your flame, you may want to set the baking sheet on top of an upturned baking sheet in order to get your cake closer to the fire.) Remove from the heat.

Place a scoop (about 1½ tablespoons) of the ganache in each of six small bowls and top with a sprinkle of gray salt. Place a piece of cake on top of the ganache in each bowl and cover with a few generous spoonfuls of whipped cream. Dust with cocoa powder and serve.

Sesame Ganache

Makes 4 cups

1½ gelatin sheets
½ cup (120 ml) milk
¾ cup (180 ml) heavy cream
1 teaspoon light corn syrup
5 ounces (150 g) 32% chocolate
    (milk chocolate), finely chopped
1½ cups (about 300 g) sesame seeds,
    ground in a spice grinder

Bloom (soften) the gelatin in a bowl of cold water for 20 minutes. Squeeze the water out of the gelatin and set it aside on a plate.

Combine the milk, heavy cream, and corn syrup in a medium saucepan and bring to a boil. Remove from the heat and add the gelatin and then the chocolate, and stir everything together until the gelatin dissolves and the chocolate melts. Use an immersion blender to blend the ganache until very smooth.

Stir in the sesame seeds. Cover with plastic wrap, pressing it against the surface of the chocolate to prevent a film from forming, and refrigerate until chilled and set. The ganache can be refrigerated for up to 5 days.

Chocolate Cake

Put the chocolate in a large heatproof bowl.

Combine the sugar, water, and butter in a large saucepan and bring to a boil, stirring to dissolve the sugar. Pour the mixture over the chocolate and stir to melt the chocolate, then let cool.

Preheat the oven to 325°F (165°C). Line a 9-by-13-inch baking pan with parchment paper.

Whip the eggs in a large bowl until fluffy. Fold into the chocolate mixture until thoroughly combined. Pour the batter into the lined baking pan. Put the pan in a larger baking pan and put the pans in the oven, then carefully pour enough warm water into the larger pan to come halfway up the sides of the cake pan. Quickly cover the whole assembly with foil, crimping the edges against the edges of the large pan, and bake for 90 minutes, or until you can touch the top of the cake without any batter sticking to your finger. Carefully remove from the oven and let the cake cool in the water bath.

When ready to serve, cut the cake into 12 squares. You will need 6 squares for the dessert; the remaining cake can be kept in an airtight container in the refrigerator for up to 5 days.

Makes one 9-by-13-inch cake; serves 12

1 pound (450 g) 85% chocolate, finely chopped
2 cups (400 g) sugar
⅔ cup (160 ml) water
½ pound (2 sticks; 225 g) plus 2 tablespoons unsalted butter, cut into chunks
6 large eggs

Parsnip Gelato with Caramel

Not to name-drop, but David Letterman was once served this and exclaimed, "Parsnip ice cream! Now you're just showing off." Little did he know that a fellow Midwesterner, Jake Nemmers, one of our chefs de cuisine, had come up with the dessert. We could actually pass it off as a lighter, fresher vanilla-caramel swirl.

Serves 6

For the Ganache
10½ ounces (300 g) 32% chocolate (milk chocolate), roughly chopped
3 gelatin sheets
1¾ cups (420 ml) heavy cream
¾ cup (180 ml) milk
2 teaspoons glucose

1½ cups (350 g) Parsnip Gelato (recipe follows)
½ cup (50 g) Caramelized Sesame Seeds (recipe follows)
Gray salt
Freshly ground black pepper

Make the ganache:
Preheat the oven to 350°F (180°C).

Spread the chocolate on a parchment-lined baking sheet and slide into the oven. Cook, stirring every 5 minutes, for 20 minutes or so, until the chocolate is a deep brown, the color of coffee beans. It will dry out a bit as it cooks; that's okay. Transfer to a large heatproof bowl.

Meanwhile, bloom (soften) the gelatin sheets in a bowl of cold water for 20 minutes, then squeeze out the water and set aside.

Bring the cream and milk to a boil in a medium saucepan. Pour the hot milk and cream over the chocolate and add the gelatin and glucose. Let sit for 2 minutes, then blend with an immersion blender until smooth. Cover and chill in the fridge overnight.

Just before serving, pull the gelato from the freezer and allow it to soften for 10 minutes or so. Put the sesame seeds in a small shallow bowl.

To serve, roll a generous spoonful of the ganache in the sesame seeds and place it in the bottom of a small bowl. Repeat to make a total of 6 servings. (You will have leftover ganache, which will keep for a week.) Top each ganache ball with a scoop of gelato and garnish each portion with a sprinkle of gray salt and a few cracks of black pepper.

Parsnip Gelato

Makes 1½ quarts

1½ pounds (680 g) parsnips, peeled
2 cups (480 ml) milk
⅓ cup (80 ml) heavy cream
3 tablespoons glucose
2½ tablespoons nonfat milk powder
2 teaspoons ice cream stabilizer
½ teaspoon kosher salt
⅓ cup (70 g) sugar

Steam the parsnips for 7 to 10 minutes, until softened.

Transfer the parsnips to a tall narrow container, add 1 cup (240 ml) of the milk, and blend with an immersion blender (or use a high-speed blender, such as a Vitamix). Strain through a fine-mesh sieve into a bowl, using the back of a spoon to push the mixture through. You should have just under 2 cups (445 g).

Combine the remaining 1 cup (240 ml) milk, the cream, glucose, milk powder, stabilizer, salt, and sugar in a large saucepan and heat over medium heat, whisking to combine the powders with the liquids, until the mixture reaches 180°F (82°C). Remove from the heat and transfer to a blender. Add the parsnip puree (you may have to do this in two batches, depending on the size of your blender) and blend well. Let cool.

Churn the parsnip mixture in an ice cream maker according to the manufacturer's instructions. Transfer to a freezer container and freeze.

Caramelized Sesame Seeds

Makes about 2 cups

½ cup (100 g) sugar
½ cup (120 ml) water
1 cup (225 g) sesame seeds

Prepare a parchment-lined baking sheet. Heat the sugar and water in a wide saucepan over medium-high heat, stirring to dissolve the sugar, until the mixture just begins to bubble. Add the sesame seeds and stir constantly for 5 to 10 minutes, until the liquid evaporates and the seeds become powdery and just barely golden. Working quickly, transfer the seeds to a baking sheet to cool, then store in an airtight container; they will keep for a few weeks, and you'll want to put them on everything.

Sweet Potato and Vanilla

I hear it's good to make enthusiastic statements in cookbooks. While I have been somewhat hesitant to do so throughout this one, I will say that this dessert we serve is my absolute favorite, even if David Tanis says he doesn't like it. The idea: a Mont Blanc made with roasted sweet potatoes instead of chestnuts.

Prepare the sweet potato:
Preheat the oven to 350°F (180°C).

Rub the sweet potato with olive oil and about a teaspoon of salt. Prick with a fork, put on a small baking sheet, and bake for 1 to 1½ hours, until the potato is totally soft all the way through. Let cool.

Peel the sweet potato, halve it lengthwise, and cut each half into fourths. You need about ½ cup (85 g) chunks of potato for this dessert; reserve the rest in the refrigerator for another use.

Make the rum syrup:
Combine the sugar and water in a small saucepan and bring to a boil, stirring to dissolve the sugar. Let cool.

Combine the syrup with the rum. Put the cake pieces into a bowl, pour the syrup over them, and set aside.

Make the toasted flour:
Preheat the oven to 350°F (180°C).

Put the flour in a small baking pan and toast in the oven for 18 to 25 minutes, or until it has slightly darkened in color and smells toasty. Remove from the oven.

Put a 3½-inch ring mold on a dessert plate and place 5 or so pieces of the rum-soaked cake in the mold.

Put the ice cream in a metal bowl and use a spatula or metal spoon to mix in ½ cup (85 g) of the sweet potato chunks. Use this to top the cake in the ring molds, leveling off the ice cream with the back of a knife. Remove the ring mold and repeat to make 5 more servings. Dust the desserts with the toasted flour and serve.

Serves 6

For the Sweet Potato
1 medium red sweet potato
   (with white flesh)
Extra-virgin olive oil
Kosher salt

For the Rum Syrup
3 tablespoons sugar
2 tablespoons water
¼ cup (60 ml) dark rum
½ Golden Yellow Cake (recipe follows),
   broken into 1-inch pieces

For the Toasted Flour
¼ cup (35 g) all-purpose flour

1½ cups (350 g) Vanilla Ice Cream
   (recipe follows)

Golden Yellow Cake

Preheat the oven to 350°F (180°F). Line a quarter sheet pan or a 9-by-13-inch baking pan with parchment paper.

Whip the egg whites and ⅔ cup (133 g) of the sugar in a stand mixer fitted with the whisk attachment until stiff peaks form, about 5 minutes. Transfer to another bowl (unless you have a second bowl for your stand mixer) and set aside.

Whip the yolks with the remaining ⅔ cup (132 g) sugar in the stand mixer just until fluffy, about a minute.

Whisk together the flours, baking powder, and salt in a large bowl. Gently fold in half the egg whites and half the egg yolk mixture with a rubber spatula until fully incorporated, then fold in the rest of the whites and the yolk mixture. Whisk together the water and olive oil, then slowly stream into the batter, stirring gently.

Pour the batter onto the prepared sheet pan. Bake for 12 minutes, then rotate the pan 180 degrees and bake for 12 more minutes, or until a cake tester inserted into the center comes out clean. Remove from the oven and let cool in the pan.

You need half the cake for this dessert. Cover the remainder and store until you succumb to temptation.

Makes one 9-by-13-inch cake

5 large eggs, separated
2 large egg whites
1⅓ cups (265 g) sugar
1¾ cups (255 g) all-purpose flour
⅓ cup (50 g) rye flour
2½ teaspoons baking powder
½ teaspoon kosher salt
⅔ cup (160 ml) water
¼ cup (60 ml) plus 2 tablespoons
  extra-virgin olive oil

Vanilla Ice Cream

Set up an ice bath. Combine the milk, cream, milk powder, salt, glucose, invert sugar, and vanilla bean seeds and pod in a large saucepan and bring to a boil over medium-high heat, whisking to dissolve the milk powder. Meanwhile, whisk together the granulated sugar and egg yolks in a bowl until well blended and fluffy.

Once the milk mixture comes to a boil, remove it from the heat and whisk ¼ cup (60 ml) of the mixture into the egg mixture to temper it, then whisk in another ¼ cup (60 ml). Return the tempered eggs to the saucepan and heat over medium heat, stirring constantly to make sure the eggs don't curdle, until it reaches 180°F (82°C). Immediately remove from the heat and strain through a fine-mesh sieve into a bowl. Set the bowl in the ice bath and let cool.

Transfer the ice cream base to an ice cream maker and churn according to the manufacturer's instructions. Transfer to a freezer container and freeze.

Makes 2 quarts

2¼ cups (530 ml) milk
1 cup (240 ml) heavy cream
⅓ cup (75 g) nonfat milk powder
½ teaspoon kosher salt
3 tablespoons glucose
2½ tablespoons invert sugar
1 vanilla bean, split lengthwise and seeds
  scraped out
¼ cup (50 g) granulated sugar
8 large egg yolks

Candied Squash and Cream Cheese Ice Cream

When I was a kid, I never quite understood why my grandmother pickled squash for her preserves, but over time, I've realized that it both makes the squash crunchy on the outside and soft within and deepens its natural caramel flavor. We would usually eat the preserves with a farmer's cheese. The addition of *alfajores*, the flaky pastry I also grew up eating, helps round out the cold ice cream.

Practical Note: The pickling lime allows you to cook the squash all the way through, so that it's very soft on the inside, but still firm on the outside. If you don't use it, you'll end up with squash mash. You will need to soak the squash for 12 hours before candying it.

Make the squash:
A day before you want to candy the squash, soak it in a pickling lime solution. The lime is caustic and can be dangerous, so wear gloves and make sure you are very careful when working with it. You'll need 1 tablespoon pickling lime for every 9 ounces (250 grams) of squash—roughly 1½ tablespoons for half an average-sized squash. Dissolve the pickling lime in enough water to cover the squash, then submerge the squash and let sit for 12 hours at room temperature (make sure it is out of reach of children), stirring it every hour or two.

The next day, drain the squash and rinse under cold running water for 10 minutes to make sure all the pickling lime is washed away.

Combine the water and sugar and bring to a boil, stirring to dissolve the sugar. Add the squash and clove, reduce the heat, and simmer gently for 2 to 2½ hours, until the squash is nearly translucent and the liquid has reduced by half. Let cool.

Remove the squash from the syrup, chop into 1-inch cubes, then return to the syrup. Refrigerate until needed; bring to room temperature before serving.

Make the alfajores:
Preheat the oven to 325°F (165°C). Line a baking sheet with parchment paper. Whisk the cornstarch, flour, baking powder, and baking soda together in a small bowl.

Cream the butter and sugar together in a stand mixer fitted with the paddle attachment until light and fluffy (you can also use a hand mixer). Add the rum, egg yolks, and egg white and mix to combine.

Serves 6

For the Candied Squash
½ kabocha squash (about 1 pound/
    445 g), peeled, seeded, and cut into
    2-inch chunks
Pickling lime (see Note)
6 cups (1.5 l) water
2½ cups (500 g) sugar
1 clove

For the Alfajores
Scant 1 cup (120 g) cornstarch
¾ cup (100 g) all-purpose flour
¾ teaspoon baking powder
¼ teaspoon baking soda
4 tablespoons (115 g) unsalted butter,
    at room temperature
½ cup (100 g) sugar
1 tablespoon dark rum
2 large egg yolks
1 tablespoon beaten egg white

¼ cup (60 ml) plus 2 tablespoons Cynar
Pinch of citric acid
About 2 cups (475 g) Cream Cheese
    Ice Cream (recipe follows)
Flaky salt

Add the dry ingredients in two batches, mixing just until everything comes together. Turn out the dough and roll it out between two pieces of parchment paper until ¼ inch thick.

Lift off the top sheet of parchment and transfer the dough, still on the bottom sheet of parchment, to a baking sheet. Bake for 15 to 18 minutes, or until the dough is just set in the middle; you don't want it to develop any color. Let cool completely, then break into bite-sized pieces; they will crumble in your mouth.

When you're ready to serve, mix ¼ cup (60 ml) of the squash syrup with the Cynar in a small bowl. Stir in the citric acid.

Place a 4-inch ring mold in the center of a dessert plate, arrange a layer of squash chunks—about 10 of them—in the mold, and top with 4 or 5 pieces of alfajores. Top with a layer of the ice cream, roughly ⅓ cup, and finish with a sprinkle of flaky salt. Remove the ring mold and repeat to make 5 more servings. Spoon 1 tablespoon of the Cynar syrup around the edge of each dessert, and serve.

Cream Cheese Ice Cream

Two days before you plan to make the ice cream, set a strainer over a small bowl and line it with cheesecloth. Put the ricotta in the strainer and wrap it in the cheesecloth. Find something heavy—like a small bowl with a can of beans inside of it—to weight it down. Refrigerate the ricotta for 2 days to drain.

When ready to make the ice cream, set up an ice bath. Combine the milk, cream, sugar, glucose, milk powder, and salt in a medium saucepan and bring to a boil, whisking to dissolve the milk powder. Remove from the heat.

Meanwhile, whisk the egg yolks in a small bowl until smooth. Whisking constantly, add about ¼ cup (60 ml) of the milk mixture to temper the egg yolks. Whisk in another ¼ cup (60 ml) of the mixture, then return the tempered egg mixture to the saucepan and heat, stirring with a heatproof spatula to prevent the eggs from curdling, until the mixture reaches 180°F (82°C). Remove from the heat, strain into a heatproof bowl, and set the bowl in the ice bath to cool.

Add the drained ricotta and the cream cheese to the custard mixture and blend thoroughly with an immersion blender. Transfer to an ice cream maker and churn according to the manufacturer's instructions. Transfer to a freezer container and freeze.

Makes 1½ quarts

1 cup (225 g) ricotta cheese
2½ cups (600 ml) milk
⅓ cup (80 ml) heavy cream
3 tablespoons invert sugar
1½ tablespoons glucose
⅓ cup (75 g) nonfat milk powder
½ teaspoon kosher salt
7 large egg yolks
4 ounces (115 g) cream cheese

Grapefruit and Yogurt

If you're a Campari person, you should definitely try this. And if not, you should anyway.

Serves 6

1 Meyer lemon
½ cup (120 ml) water
½ cup (100 g) sugar
¼ cup (60 ml) Campari
1½ cups (about 375 g) Yogurt Sorbet
   (recipe follows)
1¾ cups (about 435 g) Grapefruit Sorbet
   (recipe follows)
10 Meringues (recipe follows)
¼ cup (60 ml) plus 2 tablespoons Lemon
   Curd (recipe follows)

At least an hour before serving, slice the Meyer lemon into rounds about ¼ inch thick. Cut each round into 6 triangles. Transfer the triangles to a small bowl.

Combine the water and sugar in a small saucepan and heat, stirring, until the sugar dissolves. Remove the syrup from the heat and let cool.

Pour ½ cup (120 ml) of the simple syrup over the lemons. Combine the remaining syrup with the Campari in a small bowl, mixing well.

About 10 minutes before serving, remove the yogurt sorbet from the freezer to soften slightly.

Place a 3-inch ring mold in the center of a dessert plate. Spread a layer of the grapefruit sorbet in the ring, ¼ to ⅓ cup (about 70 g). Make a little well in the center of the sorbet, break up a meringue or two, and add to the well, along with a tablespoon of the lemon curd and a spoonful of the syrupy lemon slices. Top with a scoop of the yogurt sorbet, then level it off with the back of a knife. Remove the ring mold and repeat to make 5 more servings. Pour a spoonful or two of the Campari syrup around the edges of each dessert, and serve.

Sorbets

**Makes 1 quart Grapefruit Sorbet and
1 quart Yogurt Sorbet**

1 cup (240 ml) water
¾ cup (150 g) sugar
¼ cup (60 ml) glucose
1½ teaspoons sorbet stabilizer
Grated zest of 2 Ruby Red grapefruits
   (about 1 tablespoon loosely packed)
2¼ cups (540 ml) fresh Ruby Red grapefruit
   juice (from about 3 grapefruits)
Citric acid
4 cups (32 ounces/scant 1 l) full-fat
   Greek yogurt

When ready to make the sorbets, set up an ice bath. Combine the water, sugar, glucose, and stabilizer in a saucepan and heat, stirring to dissolve the sugar, until the mixture reaches 180°F (82°C). Transfer to a heatproof bowl, set it in the ice bath, and let cool.

Measure the glucose mixture and transfer half of it to a bowl. Stir in the grapefruit zest and juice, mixing well. Add a pinch of citric acid and taste; it should make your mouth pucker a little. Add more citric acid if you think it needs it.

Transfer the mixture to an ice cream maker and churn according to the manufacturer's directions. Transfer to a freezer container and freeze.

continued

Transfer the yogurt to a medium bowl. Add the remaining glucose mixture and blend with an immersion blender.

Churn the yogurt mixture in the ice cream maker. Transfer to a freezer container and freeze.

Meringues

Preheat the oven to 180°F (80°C) or its lowest setting. Line a baking sheet with parchment paper.

Whisk together the egg whites and both sugars in a heatproof bowl. Set the bowl over a saucepan of gently simmering water and heat the mixture, stirring to dissolve the sugars, until it reaches 120°F (50°C). Remove from the heat and let cool.

Transfer the egg white mixture to a stand mixer fitted with the whisk attachment and whip until the egg whites hold stiff peaks. Transfer to a piping bag (or use a zip-top bag with one bottom corner cut off) and pipe little silver dollar–sized dollops of meringue onto the lined baking sheet. Bake for 90 minutes, or until the meringues are just set but have not taken on any color.

Turn off the oven, leaving the meringues inside, and let cool completely, then transfer to an airtight container. They will keep for a week, though they will lose some crispness as the days go by.

Makes 20 meringues

4 large egg whites
⅔ cup (133 g) granulated sugar
¼ cup (50 g) lightly packed light brown sugar

Lemon Curd

Combine the butter and sugar in a medium bowl and cream with a hand mixer on medium-high speed until light and fluffy. Add the eggs and beat until combined.

Transfer the mixture to a wide saucepan and whisk in the lemon juices. Bring to a very gentle boil, stirring, and cook for 12 to 15 minutes, stirring almost constantly, until the mixture becomes slightly thick and glossy and a spatula dragged through it leaves a light trail; it will thicken once cooled. Remove from the heat. For more intense citrus flavor, stir in the lemon zest. Transfer to a bowl and let cool, then cover and refrigerate. The curd will keep for up to 1 week in the refrigerator.

Makes ½ cup

6 tablespoons (85 g) unsalted butter, at room temperature
¾ cup (150 g) sugar
2 large egg yolks
⅓ cup (80 ml) fresh lemon juice
⅓ cup (80 ml) fresh Meyer lemon juice
Grated zest of 1 lemon (optional)

Clockwise from top: **Grapefruit and Yogurt (page 279);
Strawberry and Coconut with Pickled Strawberries
(page 282); Parsnip Gelato (page 271)**

Strawberry and Coconut with Pickled Strawberries

I think that the best thing you can do with strawberries is make them into a sorbet. Anything else you do with them tends to fall short for me.

Combine the coconut milk and half the sugar in a medium saucepan and bring to a boil.

Meanwhile, whisk together the eggs, egg yolk, remaining sugar, and the cornstarch in a medium bowl. Whisking constantly, gradually add about ½ cup (120 ml) of the coconut milk mixture to the egg mixture to temper the eggs and whisk to make sure there are no lumps. Gradually whisk in the remaining coconut milk mixture. Return everything to the saucepan and bring to a boil over medium heat, stirring with a heatproof spatula to ensure even cooking, then remove from the heat. If there are any lumps, buzz the mixture with an immersion blender until smooth. Stir in the salt and let cool, then refrigerate in an airtight container. (The coconut cream can be made ahead and refrigerated for up to a week.)

To serve, put a 3½-inch ring mold in the center of a dessert plate. Spread about ¼ cup (60 g) of the sorbet evenly in the mold, then make a little well in the middle of it. Add a tablespoon of the coconut cream, a few pickled strawberries, and a sprinkle of the crushed coconut chips. Top with another layer of sorbet, spreading it evenly, and remove the ring mold. Repeat to make 5 more servings. Spoon a teaspoon or two of the strawberry pickling liquid around each dessert and serve immediately.

Serves 6

2 cups (480 ml) full-fat coconut milk
Scant ½ cup (95 g) sugar
2 large eggs
1 large egg yolk
2 tablespoons plus 1 teaspoon cornstarch
Pinch of kosher salt
1½ cups (about 360 g) Strawberry Sorbet
 (recipe follows)
½ cup (150 g) Pickled Strawberries
 (recipe follows), plus 2 tablespoons
 of the pickling liquid
1 cup (90 g) toasted coconut chips
 (we use Dang brand), lightly crushed

Pickled Strawberries

Combine the water, both vinegars, the sugar, peppercorns, cinnamon stick, and clove in a medium saucepan and bring to a boil, stirring to dissolve the sugar. Let cool completely.

Put the strawberries in a jar big enough to hold 2 cups (480 ml) liquid, then pour over the cooled vinegar mixture. Make sure the strawberries are completely submerged. Chill in the refrigerator overnight before serving.

Makes about 3 cups

⅓ cup (80 ml) water
¼ cup (60 ml) white vinegar
¼ cup (60 ml) red wine vinegar
1¼ cups (250 g) sugar
½ teaspoon black peppercorns
½ cinnamon stick
1 clove
12 ounces (340 g) strawberries,
 hulled and trimmed of any green
 and white parts

Strawberry Sorbet

Makes about 1½ quarts

6 cups (about 850 g) chopped
    strawberries
1 cup (240 ml) water
¾ cup (175 g) sugar
¼ cup (60 ml) glucose
1½ teaspoons sorbet stabilizer
Pinch of citric acid

Puree the strawberries in a blender, then pass through a fine-mesh strainer into a bowl.

Combine the water, sugar, glucose, and stabilizer in a small saucepan and heat, stirring to dissolve the sugar, until the mixture reaches 180°F (82°C). Let cool completely.

Add the cooled liquid to the strawberry puree. Add the citric acid and stir well. Transfer to an ice cream maker and churn according to the manufacturer's instructions. Transfer to a freezer container and freeze.

Pineapple Sorbet with Huckleberries

If you think about where and how the two ingredients grow, pineapples and huckleberries have absolutely nothing in common. This dessert stems from my desire to blend those two different yet complementary worlds (the same is true for the strawberry and coconut dessert on page 282, by the way). Good on their own; together much better.

Serves 6

About 2 cups (500 g) Pineapple Sorbet (recipe follows)
⅓ cup (40 g) fresh huckleberries, rinsed
3 to 4 tablespoons pickling liquid from Pickled Thai Chiles (page 295)

Makes 2 quarts

2 large pineapples, trimmed, peeled, quartered lengthwise, and cored
1 cup (240 ml) water
¾ cup (150 g) sugar
¼ cup (60 ml) glucose
1½ teaspoons sorbet stabilizer

Place a ring mold in the center of a dessert plate and spread about ⅓ cup (80 g) of the sorbet in the mold. Lift off the mold and repeat to make 5 more servings. Sprinkle the huckleberries around the edges of the sorbet, then follow them with about 2 teaspoons of the chile pickling liquid. Serve immediately.

Pineapple Sorbet

Preheat the broiler to high, with the rack set as close as possible to the flame. Arrange the pineapple on a baking sheet and place under the broiler. (You may have to place the baking sheet on top of another upside-down baking sheet to get it close enough to the flame.) Broil, turning it every few minutes to char evenly, until nicely charred, 5 to 10 minutes, depending on how strong your flame is. Let cool.

Cut the pineapple into 1-inch chunks.

Set up an ice bath. Combine the water, sugar, glucose, and stabilizer in a saucepan and heat, stirring to dissolve the sugar, until the mixture reaches 180°F (82°C). Transfer the glucose mixture to a blender, add the charred pineapple chunks (you may have to do this in two batches, depending on the size of your blender), and blend until as smooth as possible. Pour into a heatproof bowl and set the bowl in the ice bath to cool.

Transfer the mixture to an ice cream maker and churn according to the manufacturer's directions. Transfer to a freezer container and freeze.

stocks
and pic

Our stocks are quite versatile. The chicken stock is made into a jus for many preparations, such as quail and pork: Instead of reducing in a traditional manner, we keep it brothy and adjust with ingredients like green garlic juice and vinegar to fit different recipes. Meanwhile, the ham stock is great for certain seafood. Others, like the mushroom and squid ink stocks, serve

ckles

very specific purposes at the restaurant but could easily be used in more ways at home. I suggest you store your stocks in quart containers in the freezer.

You could certainly snack on these pickles, but you'll notice that aside from the carrots (which are actually a snack; see page 58), we usually use these as ingredients in various dishes.

Chicken Stock

This is probably the smartest one to keep in your freezer.

Preheat the oven to 400°F (200°C). Line two rimmed baking sheets with wire racks (if you don't have racks, line the sheets with foil).

Lay the thighs on one baking sheet and as many wings as you can fit on the other (you'll have to cook the wings in two batches). Roast them until they are a nice deep golden brown, 45 to 60 minutes, flipping the wings halfway through. The thighs will take a little less time. Be careful when handling the baking sheets, since the rendered fat will be hot and messy. Remove from the oven and let cool. Arrange the remaining wings on a rack on a baking sheet and roast them; let cool.

Put the wings and thighs in a large stockpot, add the water, and bring it just to a simmer, skimming off the fat as it rises. Simmer gently, skimming frequently, for 6 hours, uncovered; you just want to see a bubble every few seconds. Remove from the heat and let cool slightly.

Pour the stock through a colander into a large container, then strain through a fine-mesh sieve into another container. Refrigerate overnight, then skim off the congealed fat with a large spoon, removing as much of it as you can. The stock can be refrigerated for 4 to 5 days or frozen for up to 6 months. If you freeze it, make sure to leave a little room in your containers to allow it to expand; or, to save space, freeze it in freezer bags on a flat surface in the freezer.

Makes about 2 quarts

2 pounds (900 g) chicken thighs
8 pounds (about 3.5 kg) chicken wings
4 quarts (about 4 l) cold water

Chicken "Jus"

We'll use chicken jus to finish most of our pork and quail dishes. You may also want to try it with chicken or duck. To prepare this jus, you'll reduce the stock and reinforce it with vin jaune (or any other oxidized wine), sherry, and green garlic juice. But at home, you can experiment: Use brandy or whiskey instead of the vin jaune, and even incorporate different vinegars. It's really up to you. Just remember that you don't want to cook it down to stickiness—or mute the qualities of the alcohol.

Makes about 1¾ cups

3 cups (700 ml) Chicken Stock
   (opposite page)
2 tablespoons vin jaune or any oxidized
   wine, such as oloroso sherry
1 tablespoon sherry vinegar
1½ teaspoons Green Garlic Juice
   (page 46)
Kosher salt

Put the chicken stock in a medium saucepan, bring to a simmer, and simmer for 10 minutes, until the liquid has reduced by about a third. Turn off the heat and add the vin jaune, vinegar, green garlic juice, and a pinch of salt. Taste—it should be rich and deep and punchy. Adjust the seasoning to taste.

Fish Stock

Two types of fish, black bass and red snapper, make the best stock. It's fishy in the right way, with defined edges. It would be great in risottos, pastas, and stews. If you'd like the flavor of the stock to be stronger, you can just reduce it a bit, but be careful, as that is not my preference.

Makes 2 quarts

4 pounds (1.8 kg) head-on red snapper or
   black bass carcasses, stripped of any
   remaining flesh
3 quarts (2.8 l) water

Preheat the oven to 400°F (200°C).

Arrange the fish carcasses on parchment-lined baking sheets and roast for 20 to 30 minutes, just until they get a bit of color on them. You don't want them to get too dark; that would give your stock a bitter flavor.

Transfer the carcasses to a large stockpot and cover with the water. Bring just to a gentle simmer, making sure not to let the water boil, and simmer gently for 1 hour. Remove from the heat and let cool.

Pour the stock through a colander into a large container, then strain through a fine-mesh sieve into another container. The stock can be refrigerated for up to 3 days or frozen for up to 1 month.

Squid Ink Stock

Our Fried Arroz Negro (page 97) calls for you to infuse the rice with this stock, which should taste like you've jumped into the ocean and swallowed a bit of water and might even drown. Like our fish stock, it's great in risottos, pastas, and stews.

Pour the stock into a medium pot, add all the dried seafood, and bring just to a simmer, then let simmer gently for 45 minutes.

Strain the stock into a deep container. Add the fish sauce, squid ink, and xanthan gum and blitz with an immersion blender until you have a smooth, dark stock. Let cool. The stock can be refrigerated for up to 3 days.

Makes 2½ cups

4 cups (scant 1 l) Fish Stock (page 289)
1¾ ounces (50 g) dried squid (5 squid)
Generous ¼ cup (30 g) dried clams
¾ cup (about 100 g) dried scallops
¾ cup (40 g) dried anchovies
½ cup (60 g) dried mussels
⅓ cup (30 g) dried shrimp
1 tablespoon fish sauce
1 tablespoon plus 1 teaspoon squid ink
⅛ teaspoon xanthan gum, for body

Kombu Butter Stock

This is our take on a Japanese kombu dashi—the savory seaweed stock that is the base of so many dishes, including miso soup—which we enrich with butter and, at the last moment, brighten with grapefruit.

Soak the dried shiitakes in a bowl of hot water for 5 minutes to purge them of any dirt. Soak the kombu in another bowl of hot water to remove excess salt. Lift the shiitakes out of the water and drain well. Drain the kombu.

Transfer the shiitakes and kombu to a large saucepan, add the water, and bring to a very gentle simmer over medium heat; don't allow the water to boil—that would cause an unpleasant acidity. Simmer for 20 minutes.

Strain the liquid through a fine-mesh sieve (discard the mushrooms and kombu) and return it to the pan. Whisk the butter into the pan in increments and melt it over very low heat. Buzz with an immersion blender until emulsified. Season with 2 pinches of salt.

If using immediately, stir in the grapefruit juice; if you're making it ahead of time, wait. The stock can be refrigerated for up to 1 week. It will separate when you store it, so you'll want to heat it in a saucepan over low heat to liquefy and then buzz it with the immersion blender before using; stir in the grapefruit juice at the last minute.

Makes 2 cups

1¾ ounces (50 g) dried shiitake
   mushrooms
Two 3½-inch squares kombu
2 cups (480 ml) water
5 tablespoons (50 g) unsalted butter
Kosher salt
A squeeze of fresh grapefruit juice
   (preferably from a white grapefruit), or
   more to taste

**1. Mushroom stock, 2. squid ink stock,
3. chicken stock, 4. ham stock**

Mushroom Stock

There are some dried shiitakes in this for depth, but the humble button mushroom does the real work in developing this earthy and sweet broth. Another good one for risotto or perhaps a pasta with mushrooms.

Heat a stockpot or large Dutch oven over medium-high heat until it's good and hot, then add a teaspoon or so of grapeseed oil, enough to just barely coat the bottom. Add the button mushrooms and toss with the salt, then add the onions and garlic to the pot. (Yes, this is a lot of mushrooms.) Cover the pot, reduce the heat to medium, and let everything sweat and soften for 8 to 10 minutes, stirring twice just to distribute the mushrooms evenly.

While the mushrooms cook, soak the dried shiitakes in a bowl of hot water for 5 minutes to purge them of any dirt. Soak the kombu in another bowl of hot water to remove excess salt. Lift the shiitakes out of the water and drain well. Drain the kombu.

Add the drained shiitakes and kombu, the peppercorns, coriander seeds, water, and bay leaves to the pot and bring to a boil. Reduce the heat to a gentle simmer—you want to see a bubble only every few seconds—partially cover the pot, and cook for 1½ hours. Remove from the heat and let cool.

Strain the stock through a fine-mesh sieve into a large container; discard the solids. The stock can be refrigerated for up to a week or frozen for up to 1 month (freeze it in small batches so you can more easily use only what you need).

Makes 1½ quarts

Grapeseed oil
4½ pounds (scant 2 kg) button mushrooms, wiped clean, then broken up by hand or thinly sliced
¾ teaspoon salt
1½ cups (225 g) chopped onions
2 large garlic cloves
4 ounces (115 g) dried shiitake mushrooms
One 3½-inch square kombu
1 teaspoon black peppercorns
1 teaspoon coriander seeds
9 cups (2.1 l) water
2 bay leaves

Ham Stock

We offer a plate of Spanish cured ham as a snack, which means that we always have discarded scraps of prized *jamón* that are too good to throw into the bin. We use them to make this stock, which is at the foundation of our monkfish dishes. It would be great to cook beans and kale in.

Makes 5 cups

9 ounces (250 g) cured ham cubes (we use Ibérico shoulder, but prosciutto would be fine, chopped)
2 dried shiitake mushrooms

Place the ham pieces in a small pot with 3 cups cold water and heat over medium-high heat. Once it comes to a boil, strain through a fine-mesh sieve and discard the water and put the ham back in the pot. This blanching process helps remove impurities that might cause your final stock to become cloudy and also reduces the

One 3½-inch square kombu
5 cups (scant 2 l) water
¾ teaspoon fish sauce
Kosher salt
Green Garlic Juice (optional; page 46)

salinity of the ham, which allows you to season the final product to your preferred level.

Meanwhile, soak the dried shiitakes in a bowl of hot water for 5 minutes to purge them of any dirt. Soak the kombu in another bowl of hot water to remove excess salt. Lift the shiitakes out of the water and drain well. Drain the kombu.

Add the 5 cups of water, shiitakes, and kombu to the pot with the ham, bring just to a simmer, and simmer very gently for 45 minutes.

The best way to check if all the flavor is extracted from the ham is to taste a ham bit. If the meat is flavorless, then it's all in the broth.

Remove from the heat and strain through a fine-mesh sieve. Season the broth with fish sauce and salt to taste. If you want a little bit more funk, add a little green garlic juice. The stock can be refrigerated for up to 1 week or frozen for 1 month.

Pickled Mushrooms

You'll encounter these mushrooms in just one recipe, the Cod with Gem Lettuce, Chanterelles, and Potatoes (page 180), but I recommend you apply them to your own recipes for other similar fish, or for chicken and quail. They work well inside a grilled cheese sandwich, adding some tang.

Makes 2 quarts

10 ounces (about 3 cups; 280 g)
    chanterelles
½ small onion, cut into short, thin strips
    (about ½ cup/50 g)
2 garlic cloves
1 teaspoon chile flakes
1 bay leaf
1½ teaspoons kosher salt
1½ teaspoons black peppercorns
2½ cups (600 ml) white vinegar
2 cups (480 ml) water
¼ cup (50 g) sugar

Rinse the chanterelles in several changes of water to remove any lingering dirt. Drain and transfer to a heatproof medium container. Add the onion, garlic, chile flakes, bay leaf, salt, and peppercorns.

Combine the vinegar, water, and sugar in a medium saucepan and bring to a boil, stirring to dissolve the sugar. Pour over the mushrooms and let cool, then refrigerate. The mushrooms will keep in the refrigerator for up to 3 months.

Clockwise from top left: Pickled ramps, pickled nettles, pickled Thai chiles, pickled mushrooms, pickled carrots

Pickled Nettles

Make sure the nettles you buy are sturdy and not wispy. And make sure to wear gloves when handling them. Pickled nettles make a good addition to a grilled cheese or steak sandwich. Or chop them to use as a filling for pasta or to make salsa verde.

Makes about 1 quart

3 heaping cups (285 g) raw nettles,
    cleaned and thick stems removed
1½ cups (360 ml) white vinegar
1 cup (240 ml) water
½ cup (100 g) sugar
½ teaspoon kosher salt

Put the nettles in a heatproof container.

Combine the vinegar, water, sugar, and salt in a medium saucepan and bring to a boil, stirring to dissolve the sugar. Pour over the nettles and let cool, then refrigerate. The nettles can be refrigerated for up to 6 months.

Pickled Ramps

When ramp season comes around, people go crazy. For me, there's no better way to enjoy them, though, than pickled. Try them on pizza or a roast pork sandwich.

Makes about 1 quart

3 pounds (1.4 kg) ramps, washed and hairy
    roots removed, leaves remain attached
1½ cups (360 ml) white vinegar
1 cup (240 ml) water
½ cup (100 g) sugar
½ teaspoon kosher salt

Put the ramps in a large heatproof container.

Combine the vinegar, water, sugar, and salt in a medium saucepan and bring to a gentle boil, stirring to dissolve the sugar. Pour over the ramps and let cool, then refrigerate. The ramps can be refrigerated for up to 3 months.

Pickled Thai Chiles

There's an unidentifiable source of heat in many of our salads that comes along toward the end of a mouthful. It's the magical liquid that results from this recipe. As a matter of personal preference, I don't eat the chiles themselves—but you can. Other uses: in cold desserts. It's actually in our Pineapple Sorbet with Huckleberries (page 285).

Makes about 3 cups

4 ounces (about 2 cups; 115 g) Thai chiles
2½ cups (600 ml) white vinegar
2¼ cups (540 ml) water
¼ cup (50 g) sugar
½ teaspoon kosher salt

Rinse the chiles and put them in a medium heatproof container.

Combine the vinegar, water, sugar, and salt in a medium saucepan and bring to a boil, stirring to dissolve the sugar. Pour over the chiles and let cool, then refrigerate. The chiles can be refrigerated for up to 3 months.

Sourcing

Here are a few resources that may be helpful. At the very least, they'll point you in the right direction if you get in touch.

Beef: Snake River Farms ships nationwide: snakeriverfarms.com; Niman Ranch ships as well; nimanranch.com; Fleishers is a favorite of shops to visit in New York that thankfully also mails its product: fleishers.com.

Cheeses: We source all of our cheeses from a great purveyor, Chris Killoran at Chef Collective. For home cooks, some good options are igourmet.com, zingermans.com, and murrayscheese.com (Murray's is an amazing New York City shop).

Dried seafood: As with red bird's-eye chiles, Chinatowns are your best bet, but there are a variety of sources online, including ustrading.com/en and filstop.com/dried-fish.

Fresh heart of palm: Puna Gardens, in Hawaii: punagardens.com.

Japanese ingredients: The Japanese Pantry: thejapanesepantry.myshopify.com. Or if you're in New York, please visit the great East Village shop Sunrise Mart, which has literally everything: sunrisemart-ny.com.

Lamb ribs: You're looking for Denver-cut spareribs, which can be ordered through D'Artagnan: dartagnan.com.

Mandarin orange olive oil: Lucero (lucerooliveoil.com) makes a mandarin orange olive oil, and the Agrumato brand, available as Agrumato Orange extra-virgin olive oil from Abruzzo is another great choice (amazon.com).

Oysters and mussels: Island Creek Oysters, a great purveyor in Maine, will send oysters, mussels, and other shellfish: islandcreekoysters.com/ico.

Pork: Flying Pigs Farm, up in Shushan, New York, offers the pork butt ideal for our main dishes and much, much more: flyingpigsfarm.com.

Quail: D'Artagnan can deliver 4-ounce quail: dartagnan.com.

Red bird's-eye chiles: Most Chinatowns and especially Thai markets should have you covered, but Temple of Thai will ship the green variety: templeofthai.com. And Bangkok Center Grocery, in Manhattan, is worth a visit.

Seafood: Two great purveyors in New York City that are worth a visit are the Lobster Place (lobsterplace.com) and Mermaid's Garden (mermaidsgardennyc.com).

Smoked whitefish: Russ & Daughters, a New York appetizing classic, ships its smoked whitefish, along with almost everything serve there, from caviar to herring to schmears to bagels and bialys: russanddaughters.com.

Spanish products: Ibérico ham, mojama, anchovies, and more can be found at La Tienda (tienda.com), a Virginia-based retailer that has been around since 1996, as well as at the local favorite Despaña, in Soho (shop.despanabrandfoods.com).

Spices, seeds, salts, grains, beans, nuts, oils, and more: The amazing East Village shop SOS Chefs is worth a visit but also ships: sos-chefs.com.

Acknowledgments

Thank you to all staff members, past and present. To Estela legends Jake Nemmers, James Hardeman, Matthew Kudry, Sam Lawrence, Ryoko Yoshida, Luis Sierra, Zach Zeidman, Fabiola Escobosa, Alex Kueas, Carlos García, Michelle Capor, José Valdéz, and David Landgraf. To Isaac Flores, David Muñoz, Gonzalo Morelos, and Antonio "el Chino" González: the cooks and porters who work very hard in the back, year after year, that no one usually sees or hears.

To our determined, driven force of an editor, Ann Bramson, and to Lia Ronnen, Zach Greenwald, Renata Di Biase, Michelle Ishay-Cohen, and the rest of the team at Artisan for their willingness to go on a journey with a couple of rookies. To my agent, Kitty Cowles, for helping to open this door. To copy editor Judith Sutton, for her knowledge and scrutiny. To Marcus Nilsson, for the great vibes and always being down to shoot it again. To the dear James Casey, for his sharpness, insight, and patience. And to Gabe Ulla, who is my brother now, and *Los Papos*, his parents.

To recipe developers Marian Bull and Caroline Lange and the pros and friends who test-drove dishes and juiced plenty of cilantro and sorrel along the way, including Ali Slagle, Elizabeth Bossin, Cybelle Tondu, Lily Mirabelle Freedman, Jay Strell, Adam Sachs, Frederico Ribeiro, Christine Muhlke, Esther Wahrhaftig, Marc Blazer, Lucas Wittmann, Alex Rialdi, Betsy Klein, Oliver Strand (sorry about your finger), Howie Kahn, and Anna Polonsky.

To Francis Mallmann, Santiago Garat, Fernando Aciar, Clo Dimet, Federico Desseno, Paola Carosella, Juliana López May, and all the friends and cooks who were there at the beginning and have stuck around. To my older brother Gilbert Pilgram, the most disciplined and the most fun person in the room. To Alice Waters, for her generosity. To David Tanis, for all the wizard moves. To Chad Robertson, always there. To Gabriela Cámara, for her fullness of spirit. To Bo Bech, for speaking his mind and showing his support. To Donna Lennard, for giving me a shot in New York. And to Todd Selby and Danielle Sherman, who were some of the first people in this city to believe in me.

To Thomas Carter and Alex Vallis. You're my family.

Finally, to Paco Plater-Noya, Gabi Plater, and Sue Liguori, for endless and countless reasons.

Index